I FOUGHT THE LAW

by
PETE BITE

Skinny Songs

PUBLISHING

For my aunt Ena

Book design Belmin Pilevneli

Pete Bite is a singer/songwriter who has signed to Rak Publishing, Bron Publishing, EMI Records, Loose Records and Skinny Songs Publishing.

Also by Pete Bite
Stage plays 'Snakes and Causeways' and 'Tim and Jim'.
Short films (written & directed by Pete Mahon) 'Audition', 'Puff', 'Dead flowers can dance', 'Intruder', 'Blind date' 'Little Steve goes to the Giants Causeway' and 'Yourself'.
Short story 'If I had a hammer' written by Peter Mahon

Pete Bite music can be found at: www.petebite.com or www.petebitemusic.com

Thank To

Jim and Shirley Bradford

Maurice McElroy

Simon Groom

John Hooper

Lyn and Neville Whitton

Gerry Tweedie

Clare Phillips

Caolan and Jenna Mahon

Maureen Mahon

Masako Yano

Lawrence Jegede

Sir Mike Penning MP

Steve Latner

Brick Lane Book Group

Cathy Harris

Andrew Titcombe

Bernie O'Connor

Mark Rodgers

Denis McCann

Brendan O'Neill

Bobbie Hanvey

Lotte Daley

Jim Fitzgerald

CONTENTS

I   I FOUGHT THE LAW

PROLOGUE

This is a story that could happen to anyone though I never thought it would happen to me.

I didn't take much notice of the police when I was growing up and there was never any reason for our paths to cross. This might be considered unusual bearing in mind I grew up in Belfast and lived in an environment where police and rioters were fighting in the streets during the 1970's and 1980's. I could have been in the middle of those rioting mobs throwing petrol bombs and shouting obscenities at the police, but I never really had a reason or inclination to riot against the Royal Ulster Constabulary (RUC). I just wanted to play music. I was a musician and loved what I did. However, on one occasion I did have the misfortune to stumble into a riot with three of my friends, Jimmy O'Hare, Noel Killops and Kenny Brewster.

We were driving down the Falls Road on a hot August evening around midnight, mainly because we were bored teenagers and had a naive curiosity that got the better of us to go to the troubled areas of Belfast to have a nosey. I was the one who made the stupid decision because I was driving the car we had hired. We suddenly saw an angry mob coming towards us with bricks and sticks in their hands, so I quickly drove off the main road into a side street because I was frightened the car would get damaged. I turned again into another street only to be confronted by a line of police in riot gear. The police dragged us from the car and threw us up against a wall. With our arms stretched and our legs spread we had guns rammed into the back of our heads. They were angry and we were frightened and nothing we said was believed. It didn't matter how hard we pleaded, giving excuses for why we were there; they still insisted we were part of the rioting mob.

"We only came to look," I cried.

"Fucking liar!" screamed the copper as he pushed the gun harder and harder into my neck.

My legs started shaking uncontrollably and I just kept thinking, "this is it, I'm going to die." I had never experienced my legs shaking so much like soggy jellies, wobbling in every direction and they just wouldn't stop. He screamed and yelled and shoved his gun so hard into me I started to cry. I was frightened and confused and said the first thing that came into my head, though I was also conscious enough to try not to say anything incriminating. The dilemma lasted what seemed like hours and eventually we persuaded the police to release us. We left the scene terrified at the thought of what could have happened. That was when I decided it was time for me to leave Northern Ireland.

My real name is Peter Mahon and the pronunciation of my surname (the H-O-N bit) sounds closer to saffron or even marathon. Well maybe not quite the same as marathon, but the English insist on pronouncing it, 'hone' like cone. There is no 'e' in my surname but the English automatically say it with an 'e' on the end. Then there were those who insisted on pronouncing it May-on as in crayon. It came as a shock to me when I first arrived in England to find that people couldn't pronounce my name correctly. What I had taken for granted in Northern Ireland was destroyed when I arrived in England. So when I signed my first recording deal as a singer/songwriter I was determined to use a name that would eliminate all the confusion of the pronunciation and that's why I became Pete Bite. It sounded more Rock'n'Roll.

I left Northern Ireland to tour Scotland and then Germany with a band called 'Rico' and one day our bass player, Gerry Tweedie, while sitting in the back of the van somewhere in the Highlands of Scotland reading the New Musical Express (NME), suggested I go to London. He had just read an article about the famous record producer Mickie Most and thought it would be a good idea for me to go and play my songs to him. It might have been a dream and sometimes dreams do come true.

I arrived in London determined to meet the man who had produced more hits records than I had eaten boiled potatoes. I found his office in Charles Street just off Berkley Square and stood outside the front door, scratching my head. I had never seen a buzzer entry system before and I was puzzled as to why I heard a buzz five seconds after I had pressed the button.

"Why does it not buzz when I push the button?" I was thinking. I pushed the door but it wouldn't open. I tried again and the same thing happened. I hadn't a clue what to do but then a biker dressed head-to-toe in black leather appeared by my side.

"How do you get into this place?" I asked him.

"Just push the door when you hear the buzzer," he said, "but be quick.

You have to push while it's buzzing."

So I pressed the button and at the split second I heard the buzz, I quickly pushed the door and bingo it opened. We both entered and I headed towards reception. I told the receptionist that I had come all the way from Scotland just to meet Mr. Most. I was trying to sound polite.

"Which one?" she asked.

"Oh, are there two?"

"Yes." she replied, "David and Mickie."

"It's Mickie."

She picked up the phone, spoke to someone and then told me to take a seat and that I would be seen shortly. What a surprise! It was as easy as that and I sat in the reception not quite sure if I was really going to meet the man himself. When the office door opened I was even more surprised to see who was standing in front of me. It was the biker. "Is this Mickie Most?" I thought to myself, because I didn't have a clue what he looked like. And yes it was he. After I played him my demo tape, he offered to sign me there and then to Rak Records. The dream had come true! I wanted to believe it would happen but when it did, I was still surprised. When I went back and told Andy, the guy whose flat I was staying at off Holloway Road, he didn't believe me.

"I've been trying to sell my songs for years." he moaned, "I just don't believe you've done it after only two days in London."

I also signed with EMI, recorded in the famous Abbey Road Studios
and spent the next ten years working in the music business making a success out of a boyhood dream. Many of my songs were covered by other
singers and with the money I earned I bought the sport car I had always
dreamt about, a red MGB with a Bermuda top. I married my long-term
girlfriend Maureen, who was also from Northern Ireland; we had two
children (twins) and we bought a shop with a flat in east London. Unfortunately, Maureen and I separated years later but we still remain good
friends.

After many years I met Liz at one of my gigs in a pub in North London.
I've no idea what she saw in me but what I saw in her I thought was very
attractive. Her smile was electrifying and her intellect captivating. No
one had ever told me there are different kinds of love, and I don't even
know how many kinds there are, but I know there is the love that grows
and that was the love I had for Liz. There is also the love that fades
away and slips through your fingers. Liz was the woman I wanted but
not, as I found out years later, the woman who wanted me.

There was another side to her that I hadn't seen. Her love somehow
died and no matter what I tried to do, it could not be revived. That's
when I experienced my second encounter with the police which was not
by accident but by intention, brought about by Liz.

We bought a house in Hemel Hempstead and moved in together, but a
small dispute over money exploded into a bloody hurricane with the

police becoming involved. The situation became very scary and turned a simple matter that could have been resolved in a couple of days into an extraordinary story of confusion, conspiracy and cover-ups by Hertfordshire police that lasted for years. People like me were more trusting of professionals and more sceptical of politicians. Misperceiving that the police are honest, well does it really matter? I think it does. It shows just how deluded we are about police authorities. I feel incredibly lucky that I had the strength inside me and the willpower to take on the stress of having false allegations made against me, without letting it totally destroy me. So if you read this book as someone who has been falsely accused by the police, take heart.

The crunch of the story is, Liz told a lie to the police officers so as to have me removed from my home, thereby hoping to prevent me claiming my share of the property and that is something I will go into in more detail later. On the 14 December 2004 she arranged with PC Hughes, the offending officer, that he would remove me from my home on 19 December in the middle of the night. Hughes did not question both of us to determine the truth; he decided to turn Liz's small lie into a bigger lie, making it more believable.

Most people would expect that concrete evidence offered by both parties would be examined by police officers before any action was taken but in this case it wasn't. The fact that PC Hughes decided to write a trumped-up crime report alleging aggressive behaviour from me was a good enough reason for me to challenge the police authorities. But the more doors I knocked on for help to prove my innocence, the more doors were slammed shut in my face.

Contrary to what I had previously believed, I started to realise the police are not just unhelpful bastards but that they are a bunch of lying bastards and ever since my little encounter with them, I get an irritating feeling that every policeman I see is a liar. Deep down I know that not all cops are bent. Some do make mistakes and it's only a few that blacken the name of the police force.

My story is not a high profile miscarriage of justice but is on a much smaller scale of injustice that is not usually brought to the attention of the public. However, this kind of story happens more often than I had realised and is more common than has been publicised. There were times I found the whole experience maddening because of the many twists, turns and legal inconsistencies. What appeared to be common sense to me was distorted and destroyed by the police to make it look like there was no rhyme or reason to it.

To help demonstrate the police ineptitude, all the dialogue in this story is taken from court transcripts, tape recordings I made and letters I received. I have tried to recall as faithfully as possible what was said but the question you may be asking when you read this is, why did a simple civil matter like this turn into a criminal farce? Well, I've been asking Hertfordshire police that question for years.

So when I went to sleep on that December night in 2004 I was totally unprepared for what was about to happen.

CHAPTER 1

◇◇◇◇◇

They Can't Just Do That

I settled into my new home in Hemel Hempstead and it seemed the perfect start to a relationship that I thought would last forever. But one evening in September 2004 Liz stood in the kitchen and suddenly announced, after seven years together, that our relationship must end and I must leave the home we had bought together. I was shocked at first and when I realised she was serious I just couldn't comprehend what had come over her. She denied that she was involved with anyone else and just kept saying our relationship must finish. Why? She had no explanation.

After a painful discussion I reluctantly agreed that we would separate. I asked her if she was willing to return the money I had put into our home and at first she said "yes". But a week later after receiving advice from her brother she decided I was getting nothing. I had told her that I didn't want any part of the equity of the property but she seemed convinced that I did. There was an uncomfortable atmosphere for the next couple of weeks but we continued to live as a normal couple and I was still hoping that she would change her mind in a month or so. In an attempt to resolve our financial disagreement, I went to a solicitor to ask for advice. Even though possession was not in dispute my solicitor sent Liz a letter telling her I would not be leaving the family home until a financial agreement had been reached. He thought the letter would bring her to her senses and agree to an amicable separation. But it backfired. That's when she banished me from the bedroom to sleep on the sofa. We continued living like this for another couple of weeks, eating and sleeping separately until one night I was rudely awakened.

Suddenly the living room door was flung open, the light was switched on and I opened my eyes to see Liz looking down at me with two police officers standing behind her.

"Peter, Peter," Liz shouted, "wake-up. The police want to speak to you."

"What?" I mumbled, still half asleep.

"The police are here to speak to you."

"Oh! Why?" I asked.

There was no reply. I climbed off the make-shift bed on the sofa, looked at my watch: it was 1.30am.

"What's going on?" I said.

No one answered. I put on my dressing gown and made my way bleary-eyed towards the living room door. Had one of my relatives died or had someone been in a serious accident? The young blonde officer stood blocking my exit, his eyes glaring at me, so I stopped. Liz and the other officer were whispering in the hall. He turned to the younger officer and said, "He has to leave" and then told me to step into the kitchen.

Liz remained standing in the hall. She was a tall woman with a fuller figure, early forties and long brown hair. I noticed she was wearing a tracksuit. "That's unusual," I thought.

I had never seen her wear one before; maybe she was planning on going running? But she doesn't run and she didn't look happy.

"What's happening, Liz?"

She didn't reply. I walked into the kitchen which was at the rear of our house and only a few feet away from the living room where I was sleeping.

"What's this all about, officer?"

"I just want to ask you a few questions, Mr Ma-hone."

He couldn't pronounce my name so I made an attempt to help him. But the cocky officer just looked me straight in the eye with a grin.

"I am going to have to ask you to leave," he smiled.

"What?"

"You will have to leave immediately."

"Why?" I asked. "You can't do that."

"Oh yes we can," he continued smiling, "and if you don't go I will arrest you."

"Hang on a minute," I stuttered, "what's this all about?"

"Liz wants you out," he said.

That's when I realised Liz must have summoned the police. If this was all about our dispute over the money I had put into our home then I needed to try and explain what was happening. I told him I had a letter from my solicitor that would help clarify the situation. But before I could finish my sentence the officer interrupted,

"We don't need to see that now."

"It will help clear things up. This is a civil matter," I tried to explain.

"I have something to tell you," he whispered, "I want you to listen very carefully."

He moved closer and smiled again. I looked him in the eye.

"If you don't leave the property immediately I will arrest you. Do you understand?"

"No!" I replied.

"If you don't leave I will arrest you!"

"That's not a reason for you to arrest me," I said.

"I know Liz, and she wants you out."

"Look, let me get the letter from my solicitor and you can read it," I tried to explain again.

Then I suddenly realised what he had just said: "I know Liz." What the hell is going on here? He leaned forward and spoke closer into my face.

"I am only going to say this once more. If you don't leave immediately I will arrest you."

I stared at the floor thinking, they can't do that, can they? Then I looked up at the officer.

"This is a con, right?"

"Yes mate, you've been conned," he agreed and smiled. "Now go and get your stuff and leave! And if you want to return to the property you will need a police escort."

I rubbed my tired eyes. Where will I sleep? Work tomorrow! Four days to Christmas and I haven't bought all my presents! What absurd thoughts in the context of what was actually happening but yet it defined the reality of the situation. I may have left buying presents a little late but I never expected an eviction for Christmas. Even though the officer was determined to remove me from my home I certainly wasn't prepared, no matter how tired I was, to argue with him. He wanted some kind of confrontation but I refused to respond to the provocation. I looked up to see that the younger officer was observing from the other side of the kitchen but he didn't say a word. The smug officer moved his face closer to mine again and stared into my eyes. I looked away. Now I felt intimidated. I tried to explain that I had to get up at 6am to go to work and I was confused why I was being threatened with arrest. He was not interested that Liz and I were in the middle of a dispute about money and we were dealing with it, I suppose the way normal people deal with this kind of disagreement. I couldn't understand why the police were even involved. He continuously threatened to arrest me and I was beginning to find him annoying as he wouldn't even tell me what I was supposed to have done. It was taking all of my concentration to try and fathom out what was actually happening so I spoke slowly emphasising each syllable in case he didn't understand my Northern Irish accent. But I was wasting my time. He had a permanent grin but it was the sort of sneer that could be followed with a punch or a head-butt and the situation could very easily turn nasty. He appeared to be under some kind of instruction just to remove me with no explanation why, so I just stood there silent. I didn't ask if he had a warrant, I didn't ask if he had the authority to evict me and I didn't even ask his name or take note of his number on his lapel. I was too stunned and didn't know what to say. I kept thinking that if I kick up a stink then he might arrest me and I didn't want that to happen so I reluctantly turned and headed to go upstairs to get dressed. He followed me into the hall.

As I passed Liz on the stairs I noticed the pupils in her eyes were big and black like a cat when it's ready to pounce. I had never seen Liz like this before. I stopped and looked her straight in the face. She said nothing. I then blurted out, "Your lies will come back to haunt you Liz!" I don't know why I said it, maybe I was hoping it would make her see sense and realise what she was doing and call off the police. But she just stood motionless, staring right through me. When I saw her short statement to the police about the eviction one month later, I was shocked to see that she had claimed I'd called her "a fucking bitch" in front of the officers.

"Could you leave now, Mr Mann," shouted the smug officer from the hall.

"It's pronounced Ma-hon," I replied sarcastically as I carried on walking up the stairs.

Liz didn't flinch. She turned and walked towards the kitchen and the smug officer followed her.

What should I wear? Will I put on my work suit for tomorrow or just pull on a pair of jeans?

I was befuddled! I just didn't know what to do in this bizarre situation. Do I turn on the officers and order them out of my home or do I demand to be shown a warrant? I just didn't know, so I did nothing. The younger officer had followed me to the bedroom and was watching as I stood there in a quandary.

"Suit or jeans? Shirt or jumper?"

He continued staring as I started dressing. It felt a bit unreal and unnerving that I was being watched by a police officer putting on my underpants but the annoyance inside me helped dilute the embarrassment. Having also been an actor I was used to awkward situations of removing my clothes in front of other actors but never in an intimidating situation such as this. I had stripped in tiny dressing rooms where all my fellow actors were pulling clothes off and on practically on top of each other. No room for embarrassment with eyes looking but pretending not to. But this cop was not pretending not to, he was blatantly staring at me. I put on my dark suit that I usually wore to work. I had taken a part time job as a driver to earn some extra cash for a planned family holiday to the USA. And being a musician, playing gigs at week-ends, I didn't want to wear my gig clothes as they stank of stale smoke from the pubs I played in. Little did I know then that I would be wearing that same suit for the next six weeks without having anything else to change into.

"I'm not happy about this," I mumbled.

But the young officer said nothing. I grabbed my electric razor and stood in the bathroom trying to think of what else to take. If I packed as if I knew what I was doing, then I'd know what to pack but I didn't know what I was doing so I didn't know what to pack. I just threw some stuff into a small bag and went downstairs. I dropped the bag on the hall floor, sat on the bottom step and put my head in my hands. I still didn't understand why this was happening.

The young officer came out of the kitchen where Liz and the smug officer were and asked me for my keys.

"This is not right," I said as I handed him my bundle of keys. "Is it possible I could keep my car key or are you taking that as well?"

He reluctantly handed my key ring back and I removed the car key.

"Can you please leave now, sir," he ordered.

I opened the front door but then hesitated on the top step because just at that moment I heard Liz and the smug officer laughing aloud in the kitchen. They were rejoicing. I turned and looked at the young copper expecting a reprieve.

"Have you somewhere you can stay, sir?" he asked.

"What do you think?" I sneered. "Of course I haven't."

I looked to see if there was any sign of guilt for what he was doing to me. Maybe this was just a prank and they were having a laugh at my expense, "Sorry mate, we were only joking. Here's your keys back, come in." But no, he just told me to get out and closed the door behind me. I got straight into my car and drove off without looking back.

On 20 December 2004 I was evicted from my home in Hemel Hemp-stead at 2.30 in the morning. On that day in 1995 Prince Charles and Lady Diana divorced. What a bloody awful day for some of us!

CHAPTER 2

◇◇◇◇◇

WHAT THE HELL HAPPENED?

I went to the all-night petrol station on the approach road to the M1 and ordered a coffee. I sat looking out the window trying to comprehend what had happened. It was starting to dawn on me that I was now homeless. I only had the clothes I was wearing, the gig money that was in my wallet and a toothbrush and razor. I may not have holes in my shoes but I now have a great big hole in my world. The tears started rolling down my cheeks and as I wiped away the snot dripping from the end of my nose with the back of my hand, I felt overcome with uncontrollable crying. My body shivered with rage as I wept. I felt so betrayed and I sat questioning myself.

"What the hell has happened?"

The realisation that I had just been evicted from my home suddenly hit me. I suppose it was some kind of delayed reaction or a sudden awareness that this was not a dream. All the plans Liz and I were making had now crumbled into dust. She must have met someone else. I persuaded myself that that was her reason.

I wiped away my tears and decided to find somewhere to sleep if I was going to be able to go to work in the morning. There was a Holiday Inn Hotel next to the garage so I went into the reception and asked for a single room. The receptionist told me she had one available at £140 and it included breakfast. I looked around; the Christmas tree in the corner, the holly in the windows and the mistletoe over the counter. Maybe I should plead for a little bit of seasonal goodwill and a reduction. I only had one hundred and forty pounds in my wallet and that was it. If I spend it all on a room for the night, then I wouldn't have any money left to buy something to eat and put petrol in my car. My chequebook and Visa cards were back at my home and I had no other way of accessing money from my bank accounts, so I decided not to take the room.

I walked out of the hotel and stood wondering where to go. On impulse I drove down the M1 towards London and then pulled into the service station where I knew there was another hotel. It was £60 per night so I took it only because I was desperate and it was very cold, too cold to sleep in the car. The room was big, modern and clean and as I looked out of my first floor window I could see the frost was already starting to settle on the roof of my car. I lay on the bed and tried to sleep. I did nod off for a while but woke up again at around 6am. I decided to have a shower and a shave to try and freshen myself up. I telephoned Dave, the supervisor at the company where I had started working as a part-time driver from July 2004. I had taken the job to help save some extra money for our planned family trip the following year. My son Caolan, from my marriage to Maureen, was due to graduate from Leeds University and I thought I would surprise him with a holiday to the USA.

I began to tell Dave that I wouldn't be able to come into work as the police had kicked me out of my home. He didn't believe me and thought I was joking. Then I started to cry as all the emotion and hurt that was raging inside burst to the surface. I just didn't know what to do and I had nowhere to go. Dave then told me to take as much time as I needed to sort things out. I put the phone down and continued crying. It took me a few minutes to pull myself together and instead of going to work I decided to go to my solicitor's office in east London.

At 9am I was sitting in Ronald Fletcher Baker solicitor's reception when Mr Roberts walked in and glanced at me. I had only met him on a couple of occasions back in the 1990's so we were not on first name terms. He was a short man whose manner could be very abrupt. But he saw me immediately and took me through to his office that overlooked Old Street with the sometimes-overpowering sound of the morning rush hour traffic coming in through the open window. He refused to believe me when I told him what had happened.

"Were they real policemen?" he asked.

I told him that they were wearing uniforms and came in a police car so I assumed they were real but when he asked me if they had a warrant or documentation that's when I realised that something was amiss.

"Well, they just can't do that," he said.

He immediately turned to the bookcase behind him and pulled a book from one of the shelves and quoted section 12 of the Trust of Land and Appointment of Trustees Act 1996 which states that police officers cannot remove anyone from their home without a court order. He asked if I had their names or numbers, but of course I never thought of formal introductions and now realised I had no idea who these officers were. It was too sudden and I was too shocked to even think about exchanging names. He said he would write immediately to the Chief Superintendent of Hemel Hempstead Police and demand an explanation. He told me to go to Hemel police station to ask for the reason why I had been evicted as it would be the quickest way to find out what had happened.

I then drove to my ex-wife, Maureen's, in North London to tell her and my son Caolan and my daughter Jenna the news. They were baffled because they had always considered Liz to be a really lovely genuine person. They just could not comprehend why she would call the police. Of course I had always respected the law and those who enforced it and that was a standard my ex-wife and I had instilled into our children. We hoped they had listened. I asked Caolan to come with me to Hemel police station but first I needed to find somewhere to stay. My old friend Billy (at his request I have agreed to use a pseudonym) was only too willing to offer me accommodation in his Camden Town flat but started apologising for the mess his flat was in before I'd even seen it. I didn't think much of what he was trying to tell me over the phone, but when I got there and saw the state of his place, I was shocked. It looked like a deserted outpost in a Western movie with dust balls like tumbleweed blowing across the floor and bin bags of rubbish strewn all over the carpet, similar to an abandoned house. But I didn't care because I was so grateful to have somewhere to stay that night.

"Come in and sit down, Pete," he invited.

As he patted on the arm of the sofa to encourage me to come over I could see clouds of dust rising like smoke signals warning me I was in sneezing territory.

We stood talking in the kitchen most of that night, exchanging stories of how 'hard done by' we had both been treated by our ex-partners. He had just broken up with his partner as well, only his situation was worse than mine because there was a child involved. I slept in Billy's bed, at his request and he slept on the sofa. I felt bad about kicking him out of his bed. When I tried to sleep in it I realised that maybe he offered it to me because it was so lumpy and uncomfortable, causing me to toss and turn all night. But that didn't really matter, I just couldn't sleep anyway. There were too many questions swirling round in my head.

Taking my solicitor's advice, I drove with my son to Hemel police station on 21 December 2004 to confront the police. When we arrived at the reception desk I asked to speak to someone in authority. We were kept waiting for over two hours. I told the receptionist that we were not going to leave until someone spoke to us. Eventually a Sergeant Huffer came and took us into a quiet corridor to give an explanation.

"You were removed from the premises because there was the possibility of a breach of the peace," he stated.

"I was removed from my home," I corrected him, "and it was the police who breached my peace by waking me up!"

Even though I pointed out that I was asleep, he still maintained that it was 'possible breach of the peace'. He didn't even try to dress it up as 'actual breach of the peace'.

"And if I hadn't woken-up would it have still been possible breach of the peace because of my snoring?"

He ignored that remark and told me that I would need an escort to return to my home. I was stunned.

"But it's my home so why would I need an escort? What am I being accused of?"

"We answered a call and we were instructed to remove you from the premises," he informed me.

Who instructed him? Who gave him the authorization? The officers didn't have a warrant. But he was unwilling to divulge that information. I then told him I wanted to make a complaint about the action of the two officers but he mumbled something about being too busy. I then asked him to write down what he had just told us so I could take it to my solicitor for clarification but he insisted that under the Data Protection Act it was information he was not allowed to disclose. I stood there confused. He had told me the reason why I was removed but was now claiming he couldn't disclose that information. I just couldn't interpret what was being said or what was being implied. He made some excuse about being busy and then told us to leave.

We went outside and Caolan stood looking at me waiting for my conclusion I suppose. I was so frustrated with the sergeant's verbal garbage that I felt I had landed in a foreign country and lost the ability to understand.

"Well, what do you want to do now, Dad?"

"I don't know. Get something to eat I suppose. I'm so angry I could eat a... policeman."

CHAPTER 3

◇◇◇◇◇

Much Ado About Nothing!

I was driving out of Hemel town centre when my mobile rang. It was my cousin Clare from Downpatrick in Northern Ireland. I pulled over to explain what had happened and then started to cry. Clare started crying as well and told me not to worry.

"Whatever money you need Peter; I will send it to you immediately. I mean that, however much you need just let me know."

It was good to know that if Liz decided to stop me from withdrawing my money, which was in her account, (she did close the account a few days after my eviction) then I had the offer of some other money if I needed it. I was now discovering that solicitors were not cheap and always wanted payment up front.

My Aunt Ena, Clare's mother, had raised me since I was five when my mother died and Clare was like a big sister taking me to primary school on the Malone Road in Belfast every day. She always supported me in everything I did throughout my childhood and into my teenage years. I had ambitions to work as a television engineer and Clare found me a vacancy in a part of the country where jobs were few. I don't know how she did it but she got me a job interview with Radio Rentals in Belfast. "Never mind how I did it," she screamed, "I found you a flippin' job and you flippin' well better get it or I'll flippin' thump you!"

She had the passion to achieve and wouldn't let go of something when she got her teeth into it.

I sat in the parked car blowing my nose. The conversation with Clare had upset me. These outbursts of crying were to become more frequent over the following months.

Two days after my first visit to Hemel Police station I returned again with Caolan on 23 December to ask for the required escort I was told was necessary if I wanted to return to my home. I was desperate for a change of clothes and I also needed my gigging equipment. A young female officer was sitting at the front desk of the police station so I asked her for an escort to accompany me to my home. She looked at me with a blank expression. I explained that I had been threatened with arrest if I tried to return to my home without a police escort.

She turned to a male colleague.

"What's it for sir?" he enquired.

"To go to my home!"

"To do what, sir?"

"Collect my belongings."

"Why?"

"Because I need some clean clothes."

"Are you moving, sir?"

"No! Well yes."

We both stopped and looked at each other waiting for the other to speak. He seemed bewildered that I needed an escort and clearly amused at my request. I then raised my voice because I was not in the mood for his stupid questions but I was totally unaware of the fact that he didn't know I had been evicted. I had assumed every copper in Hemel was talking about me. He warned me about my aggression but I told him I wasn't being aggressive; I was just angry at the way the police had treated me. He told me he would need to speak to his sergeant and that's when I let out a gasp of air from my lungs to calm myself down. I gave him my real name, spelt it and pronounced it, with my address so he wouldn't get confused. He went away and then came back 15 minutes later and told me it would not be possible to have an escort because they were experiencing an outstanding workload.

I didn't believe him. That was my first clue of how unhelpful the police can be and the beginning of a pack of lies to stop me finding out the truth. In fact, I was proven correct when I contacted the local police crime analyst, six months later, asking for the crime figures for that specific date. There had only been four recorded crimes in Hemel Hempstead and none of them had occurred near the time the police officer claimed he had an 'outstanding workload'. It was all a bit of a to do about nothing. I looked the officer straight in the eye and told him to record my request for an escort. I tried to emphasise each word so as to be understood just in case he became confused because of my accent. His 'can't be bothered' attitude was annoying me and I felt like giving him a mouthful of abuse. But I didn't want my son to see his Dad behaving like an imbecile so I restrained myself, took a deep breath and spoke with a more controlled frustration. I told him I would hold him personally responsible if no officer accompanied me to my home. I threatened to make a complaint about his lack of co-operation and then I realised I didn't know his name. But he wouldn't tell me. He just repeated that they were experiencing an 'outstanding workload'. "Bullshit", I thought to myself and stood staring at him hoping he would back down. He looked young and inexperienced but yet had an air of superciliousness. I told him I would expect an officer to be at my home by 3pm. I turned and walked out.

We arrived at Adeyfield Gardens in Hemel around 2pm that afternoon and called in to see my next door neighbour John Hooper at number 16. We sat and chatted about what had happened and John told me he had seen the police arrive and leave that night. This was great news. I didn't realise there had been a witness. I asked him for a statement of what he had seen and he was only too willing to write one. Things were looking up. He was also another person who told me that the police do not have the power to remove anyone from their home; something that everyone seemed to know except me. If only I had known on the evening of the eviction maybe things would have been different but then again the two officers were preying on my ignorance. I thought that if I was arrested the officers would be forced to fabricate a reason for my arrest. How was I to know that they would fabricate a reason for not arresting me? I looked at my watch and reminded Caolan that it was time to go next door to Liz's. It was now apparent that the police were not going to send an escort.

We went next door and rang the bell. Liz opened the door and stood there surprised and silent. Her tall frame stood motionless and I couldn't determine if she was angry or sad, vindictive or sympathetic. She said nothing. I told her I had come to collect my equipment and if she wanted to phone the police I was willing to wait until they arrive. She hesitated but then agreed to let us in. I now felt uneasy stepping into the house that had been my home in which I had put so much love and work into. Her icy stare was surprisingly cooling my frustration. Caolan said he thought she was on the verge of being repentant but it didn't come across to me like that. I felt she was on the verge of throwing a wobbly. One wrong word from me and I was sure she would kick off. So I joked around to lighten the atmosphere.

I tried to look jolly but inside I had a million questions I wanted to ask. My curiosity was bursting. I was ready to explode. Why did we break-up? Why did you call the police? Why, why, why? My father always told me never to show anger so I smiled and acted the clown, but it was hard.

"I was going through our neighbour's dustbin last night", I continued talking in my jovial patter, "when the door opened and John appeared. 'What are you doing?' he asked and I told him I was looking through his bin for some food. 'Just wait there' he said and he went inside and returned with a torch."

I saw a smile start to appear on Liz's face but then she quickly dissolved it back into a frown.

We loaded the amplifiers into my car and then I told her I needed to go to my office to get some papers. I ran upstairs and she followed me. Liz's daughter was standing on the landing.

"Hello Laura, how are you?"

"Fine," she said.

The office was mainly filled with my stuff so I wasn't sure what Liz thought I was going to take. But she stood over me as I opened the filing cabinet and went straight to my bank statement folder. My papers were not in the neat order I had left them.

"Someone's been at these," I said.

"It wasn't me." she immediately snapped.

I later discovered that certain papers were missing. Receipts that would have proved I paid some of the bills. I decided to say no more. I knew she would only deny everything so I took out some documents I needed and closed the drawer. I didn't have a key to lock it so all my files were there for all to see. I grabbed a couple of presents I had hidden from Liz as I was planning to surprise her on Christmas day and offered them to her. She refused to accept them so I turned and gave them to Laura and she thanked me. Liz followed me down the stairs and stopped in the hall while I went out to the car. She stood looking at Caolan. He told me later that she didn't say a word but appeared to be on the verge of crying. I returned from the car and then Liz informed me that she had closed her bank account, the account I was paying money into for the refurbishment of our home.

"Are you going to keep that money as well?"

"When I've decided what to do I will instruct my solicitor," she stated

"Why?" I asked. "Just let me withdraw it. It is my money after all."

She didn't reply. I turned to go and noticed three new big shiny bolts on the inside of the front door.

"You're taking no chances, are you?" I joked. "Do you think I'm that desperate to get back into the house?"

She peered at me. I could have hung a curtain on that stare. Her behaviour was becoming sinister and I was not comfortable in her presence anymore. We left and drove back to London and on the return journey I kept cursing to myself, "Bugger, I've forgotten my bank cards and chequebook again!" And with all the tension in the house I had even forgotten to take some clean clothes. I just didn't know whether I was coming or going.

A few days later, I pulled up at the traffic lights near the magic roundabout in Hemel alongside a police car. I looked out of my passengers' window and noticed the driver was staring at me. I looked away and when the lights changed I drove off. I then saw in my rear view mirror a blue light flashing so I pulled over and stopped. I got out of my car and the two uniformed officers approached me. The officer who was driving pointed out that it was an offence to drive with dark glasses on. I took off my glasses and offered them, informing him that they were prescription glasses. He looked up at me, as he was considerably shorter, and told me they would restrict my vision and he could arrest me.

"So what about cars that have tinted windows?" I asked and he said the police will be taking those cars off the road as well. I looked at him and the other officer, who said nothing, and wondered if this was a joke. Of course I immediately thought that I was being picked on because of my complaint about PC Hughes and PC Thurston. "Are the police going to close every company that tints car windows?" I questioned and he agreed. I just stood there not quite sure what to say. I wanted to tell this PC what I thought of him and my anger was on the verge of flaring up to say, "What sort of a little bollox are you?" But I restrained myself and said nothing. He said I could go but told me not to wear the glasses again while driving. I ignored his warning and continued to wear those glasses.

My paranoia told me that Hertfordshire police definitely had it in for me and I should get out of Hemel Hempstead as soon as possible.

CHAPTER 4

◇◇◇◇◇

ARSE-HOLE!

Christmas day 2004 was a day I woke with a taste in my mouth that could contaminate a small country. I had endured four days of surviving on bags of chips. I smelt of vinegar soaked newspaper. I had nowhere to sleep and I just wandered around not knowing what I was doing. I didn't recognise myself when I saw the reflection of a skinny, stooping figure in shop windows. "Who is that old man? Oh that's me!" I realised. I had no access to my money and I was eating less and less - but my ex-wife Maureen, God bless her, came to my rescue and invited me for Christmas dinner.

As I sat at the Christmas Day meal with my family, I tried to put on a brave face but inside I just wanted to curl up and die. I felt terrible not having time to organize some presents or money to give to my kids. Maureen insisted I stay at her home until I sorted myself out, so that night I was pumping up the blow-up mattress to sleep on her living room floor. I couldn't get to sleep that night and as I lay there listening to the sound of the trains that ran directly behind her house, I tossed and turned. Not because of the trains but because I couldn't get the thoughts of the police actions out of my head.

On Boxing Day, I needed to get out of the house and try to collect my thoughts so I took my son's dog, Zoe, for a walk. The dog was easy to talk to and unlike some of my friends didn't call me a stupid arse-hole for having moved to Hemel. I told the dog everything because I knew she wouldn't divulge what I said but I wasn't sure if she believed me. As I sat on a park bench in Highgate fields I muttered on about Liz and the police while Zoe obediently listened. I could see in her eyes sadness as I told her my troubles but I was so immersed with my own problem that I didn't realise the dogs' sadness was not because of what I told her. She was trying to tell me that she had problems too and I was totally unaware. Two months later she was dead. She had stomach cancer. The poor thing had been suffering all the time while listening to me.

Three days later my mobile rang and I heard a woman's voice. She asked me if I was the lodger at 18 Adeyfields Gardens, Hemel Hempstead. I told her she had made a mistake that I wasn't a lodger. She then explained that Liz had told her the "lodger had moved out" and Liz had given my mobile number to settle the weekly milk bill of £6.18p. I was dumbfounded for a second and then agreed to leave the money with the next door neighbour. I couldn't believe Liz was refusing to pay. What was she trying to prove?

That same day I received another call from the next door neighbour John at number 16 telling me that Neville, who lives at the bottom of our street had offered me his spare room until 'things' were sorted out. I was surprised that so many people were willing to help and support me. I thought the removal from my home by the police might have caused people to be frightened and reluctant to get involved with a suspected criminal. It was the complete opposite. They couldn't do enough to help. Colleagues and friends from the present and the past were all willing to give me character references confirming that I was 'a rather decent chap and an all-round good egg who never used swear words.' I know it's hard to believe that someone like me who was in the music business and played in groups most of his life didn't use the 'f' word or 'c' word. It was something that was drummed into me as a kid and so I never swore. I collected about 15 letters all with glowing confirmations that I could

be trusted whatever the circumstances. But there was one friend, someone I had known and trusted for over 30 years who refused to give me
a reference. His reason was not quite clear. Whether he believed Liz or
whether he thought I was lying, I never pursued. That one refusal made
me more determined to clear my name.

I moved into Neville and Lynn's spare room the first week in January
2005, which enabled me to return to my part time job in Hemel and
work my notice. After that I felt the time would be right to leave Hemel
Hempstead and return to London. I was frightened that Liz might accuse me of stalking her or something worse. Neville and Lynn made me
feel very welcome offering me meals and the full run of their home. It
was strange living a few hundred yards down the street and yet not being
able to go into the house that had been my home for the past four years.
I never saw Liz and always tried to make sure that she didn't see me. Returning to work was difficult, as I had to explain to my work colleagues'
what had happened. One friend offered to throw a brick through Liz's
window but I told him he might as well throw me through the window
because she would know who was behind it and report it to the police.
It was nice that friends were trying to help but the kind of help I needed
was the legal kind.

My daughter Jenna told me she had written a letter and sent it to Liz. I
read it and I nearly choked on her words. She had poured her heart out
asking Liz to end this madness, which was now getting out of control.

"*My dad loved you so much,*" she wrote, "*and would have done anything to make
the relationship work. Both Caolan and I are very upset by the situation, not only*

because we can see our dad's pain but also because we felt extremely close to you. I personally viewed you like a mother and to see you do this to dad hurts me so much."

The letter brought tears to my eyes.

Liz never replied.

Liz's friend, Cathy contacted me and we sat and chatted about what had happened. Cathy told me she had gone to see Liz the day after the eviction and was shocked at the way she was behaving. She said that when Liz opened the front door the first thing she screamed was, "I got him out!" Cathy asked Liz why she had called the police but Liz refused to explain. "I had to!" Liz said and told Cathy not to ask questions like that again. None of this was making sense to me because this wasn't the Liz I had known.

A date for the court hearing to appeal for permission to return to my home was set for 12 January 2005 at Watford County Court.

Two days before the hearing I was sitting talking with Neville in his living room when the doorbell rang. It was Liz's brother Peter Palfrey. He asked to see me so Neville brought him through. Palfrey stood in the middle of the living room announcing that he was there to serve a non-molestation order on me banning me from my home and the street. He started quoting from the order while I sat there bewildered. I glanced over at Neville and he was just staring with his mouth open. Neville and Lynn's little cat was sitting in the corner, hind leg cocked, licking its bum. "What an arse-hole!" I thought as Palfrey stood reading out the order like the town crier announcing the circus was coming to town. I thought he had an exaggerated sense of his self-importance as he displayed the characteristic signs of a narcissistic politician with the common sense of a headless chicken.

"The court declares that the applicant, Mrs Elizabeth Keenan, is entitled to occupy 18 Adeyfield Gardens, Hemel Hempstead. The respondent, Mr Peter John Mahon, shall not obstruct, harass or interfere with the applicant. The respondent is forbidden to neither attend, enter or remain within, nor loiter outside or in the vicinity of the said property. The respondent is forbidden..."

I interrupted,

"But I haven't done any of those things!"

He cleared his throat and continued.

"...the respondent is forbidden to use or threaten violence against the applicant nor intimidate, harass or pester her and must not instruct..."

Neville interrupted.

"Are you a solicitor?"

Palfrey stumbled on his words and replied, "No."

"He's a magistrate," I whispered.

He continued. "…This order shall remain in force until the hearing on 12 January 2005."

He then handed me the sheet of paper and announced that I would go to jail if I did not observe the order. I asked him why he was doing this. He opened his mouth, hesitated and then said nothing.

"And why did you request the police to evict me?"

"I know nothing about the police," he claimed.

Palfrey turned and walked out and I shouted after him, "You'll be laughed out of court!"

That's what I believed when I said it and I believed that the courts would see through his ridiculous claim and this whole crazy escapade would be over in a couple of days.

But I was wrong.

CHAPTER 5

◇◇◇◇◇

BE CAREFUL MR PALFREY

On the day of the hearing, 12 January, I was still wearing the same black suit I'd had on since my eviction but I did have a clean shirt that my ex-wife, Maureen had bought me. Jenna and I arrived early and sat in the waiting room.

From the outside the building didn't look anything like a courthouse. In fact, it was a block of offices with the County Court on the third floor.

Liz appeared at the door of the waiting room with her brother Palfrey and our eyes met. She turned and walked straight out again. Palfrey came over to us and asked if I had representation.

"My barrister and solicitor haven't arrived yet," I said.

"When they arrive will you tell them I need to speak with them before we go into court?"

And he walked away. He had obviously decided to take on the responsibility of being Liz's legal representative. When my barrister, Ms Chapman, approached me to introduce herself, I noticed she was heavily pregnant.

"God, I hope she doesn't go into labour before we have the hearing," I said to Jenna.

She smiled and gave me a hardy hand shake. We went into a side room and she started discussing how she was going to conduct my case. She considered Liz's statement to be full of contradictions and thought it would hinder her claims. I stopped her and said that I didn't want to waste the court's time as I considered it to be useless to try and return to my home. I felt it would cause even more problems. Suddenly the door opened and in walked Palfrey. My barrister assumed he was my solicitor and invited him to join us. I turned to tell her that he was the opposition. He handed a letter to her and then left. The letter was from the domestic violence unit at Hemel Police station and addressed to Liz. It said that, '*police officers were called to the address in the early hours of the 20 December and found the male to be verbally abusive and aggressive.*' I sat there dazed. I didn't know what to say. This accusation of verbal aggression had never been mentioned before. I just couldn't believe what I was reading. I turned to my barrister.

"This... is... not what happened."

We went into the court. The high bench and the sectioned off seats were all in a dark wood stain and smelt of furniture polish. The court was much smaller than I had expected. The Judge appeared looking casual, shirt and tie and dressed in a tweed jacket resembling a school teacher rather than a Judge. He had no robe or wig. Only my barrister was dressed in the courtroom garments and regalia.

"Good morning to you Miss Chapman," said the Judge.

"Good morning," replied my barrister.

He then turned towards Liz and Palfrey who were without a solicitor or barrister.

"Mrs Keenan, I was prepared to deal with this the day before yesterday without your solicitors being present who, for reasons I did not go into, had sent you effectively by yourself. I am truly astonished in this application that you are not represented and you have no legal representation with you this morning."

Liz and Palfrey looked shocked.

"I have… solicitors," stuttered Liz.

"Well where are they? This is a hearing," shouted the judge.

Liz and Palfrey looked at each other and said nothing. It became clear that Palfrey had decided to appear without a solicitor. A decision that the judge didn't find favourable.

"The difficulty is that since you are in person, without representation, it might be seen that I am taking your side. But you can tell your solicitor from me that I am most unhappy (a) that they sent you the day before yesterday, and (b) that they have sent you today. In neither case was it appropriate in my view. If you have got solicitors, they should be here."

Palfrey stood up.

"Your Honour, my sister has asked me to speak for her or to represent her and that is why her solicitor is not…"

"Yes, but do be careful Mr Palfrey because what I read indicates that you are a witness of fact. I have to be careful what I allow you to do. Whatever is before the court, it is the return day of an Order that I made without Mr Mahon being present."

My barrister heaved herself up.

"Your Honour, there is no evidence before the court that Mr Mahon has threatened violence against Mrs Keenan. He is concerned about the non-molestation order being contained at all and the court should know that he doesn't accept that the incident alleged has taken place."

"Well, all I can do is to go on the evidence that I have got, and that is that the police first came to the premises but were discouraged from removing him. Then they returned on the 20th and physically removed him. That is what I have been told."

I couldn't believe what I was hearing. Who told the judge that? I strongly suspected Palfrey was behind it. I spent months making enquiries in Watford court, looking through all the statements and documents but nowhere, not even in the judge's notes could I find an explanation or even a mention of who had told the judge that I had been physically removed from my home. But when I received a copy of the court transcript of the application that Liz and Palfrey had made for the non-molestation order on the 10 January, there it was in black and white. '*He was physically removed for abusive behaviour.*' That's what Palfrey had told the judge.

This whole thing was now turning into a pantomime. I felt like jumping up and shouting, "It's not behind you, its right in front of you. Look at the evidence!" But the evidence before the judge was not in my favour. The police had made a crime report claiming I was verbally aggressive, Liz had claimed I was verbally threatening towards her and Palfrey was claiming I was physically abusive. The evidence was well and truly stacked against me and my evidence was just my version of the incident. My neighbour, John Hooper's statement, was not even considered.

"Mr Mahon saw that letter from the police for the first time this morning," stated Ms Chapman, "and it would appear that it is double hearsay and is not a first-hand account by an officer. He certainly doesn't accept that he was being abusive or aggressive."

"That as may be, but I am obviously not going to be in a position to hear oral evidence this morning," replied the judge.

"Mr Mahon has instructed me to tell the court that he has not acted in this way and he is not intending to act in this way."

Palfrey interrupted again.

"May I just add your Honour that the information in the letter from the Domestic Violence Unit does come from a PC and she has actually taken the details from the Police Log at the police station."

"Well, that's as may be," said the judge, "but I have not seen this letter."

My barrister handed the judge the letter. I was starting to wonder how

Palfrey knew so much about how the police letter came about. We all waited while the judge read the letter.

When I saw his statement, 4 years later in 2009, which Palfrey had given to the police, it stated that he had advised Liz to make a complaint about me. And when I read the police crime report it stated that Palfrey and Liz had gone to Hemel police station on 14 December 2004 to make enquiries on how to have me removed from my home. Liz had predicted a 'breach of the peace' five days before I was evicted. She was not **reporting** a crime but **predicting** a crime would occur when the police come to evict me.

"The alternative is that Mr Mahon could give me an understanding and promise to stay away from the house or else he will go to prison," announced the judge.

"This just gets better and better," I mumbled and shook my head. "Now they're telling me I will go to prison if I go to my home to collect my belongings."

"What are you going to do, dad?"

What could I do? I sat there feeling disgusted at a system that appeared to just listen to any piece of crap it was told. Then the judge turned to Liz and told her that her solicitors would have to file her evidence and there would be mutual disclosure. Palfrey stood up again.

"Could I have clarification of mutual disclosure?" asked Palfrey.

"It is the solicitors who will deal with that and not you, Mr Palfrey."

Palfrey looked embarrassed and sat down.

After we left the court my barrister informed me that Mr Palfrey had approached her in the corridor to tell her, 'off the record' as he said, that the Peabody Trust (the freeholder of the property of which I owned the lease, that I had bought in 1988) 'had phoned him' and that was all. He said nothing more. "What does he mean by that?" she asked. I wasn't sure but then later realised what he was doing.

I had rented my flat to tenants when I moved to Hemel to live with Liz. Palfrey was now trying to accuse me of illegally living with Liz in Hemel Hempstead. This was the dark side of Palfrey's behaviour coming to the surface and I was finding it very scary the way he twisted the truth.

Ms Chapman then informed me that Liz would not allow me to collect my belongings from the house until 23 January.

"What!"

"She cannot accommodate you until then," announced the barrister, "but she did say she would pack all your belongings into bin bags to speed things along."

"No! There is expensive equipment that only I know how to dismantle," I insisted. "It would speed things along if I could go and get my clothes tomorrow instead of having to wait another two weeks."

"She won't allow that."

"This is crazy," I said. "Can she do that?"

No one answered.

Two weeks later, I arrived at Adeyfield Gardens and sure enough Liz had packed all my clothes into black bin bags, piled them in the hall and had locked all the bedroom doors. Her ex-husband Steve was there and so was her daughter, Laura. I had Chris, my labourer friend who helped me do a lot of the building work around the house, and Hughie, a friend of my ex-wife Maureen. Liz refused to let me check all the rooms. I suggested to her in front of everyone that we should sit down and talk but Liz said "no". I pointed out that talking would save both of us money. She was not interested and then mumbled that she had "already made me an offer". I told her that I had not received any offer and so asked how much it was. "I'm not saying in front of these people." And off she stormed.

When I spoke to my solicitor a couple of days later he confirmed that no offer had been made. Liz said a lot of things that never materialised. She promised to forward all my mail to my London address and give my mobile number to whoever rang the house phone. But none of that happened. She returned all my letters to the senders, sent back a birthday card that had come from my friend Christie in America and returned a wedding invitation from Ireland. I couldn't understand why she was acting so vindictive or what point she was trying to make.

It took two trips from Hemel to London and it was a long hard day for all of us. When we finished loading the van for the second time I went into the house to say goodbye to Liz and Laura. They were sitting on the sofa in the living room, Laura looking shocked and Liz looking angry. I said goodbye to Laura and I wanted to give her a big hug but Liz was holding her so tight, she wouldn't let go. Then I said goodbye to Liz but she didn't reply.

It was a sad moment, leaving the woman I thought had loved me and had changed my life in so many ways. I didn't know what to do or say to her. Chris later told me that Liz had approached him to get his telephone number. I was surprised.

"Maybe she wants you to finish the work I've started."

"No," he said. "She doesn't want me to make any statements about the work I've done."

Hughie just couldn't understand why Liz's ex-husband Steve was there.

I discovered later that it was Palfrey who had phoned the manager of Peabody requesting a letter and a copy of my lease which he intended to show in future court proceedings, claiming I was living illegally in Hemel Hempstead and illegally renting my flat. How on earth he persuaded the manager to write this letter, God only knows. I phoned Peabody and pointed out to the manager in question, Mr Barnett, that my lease on the flat does not restrict me to where I live and did allow me to rent. He apologised and agreed to withdraw the letter he had sent to

Palfrey. I realised I was going to have a real battle on my hands with Palfrey trying devious means to undermine me and blacken my character. He was using coercive control over Liz that was working in an insidious way but nevertheless deadly.

Palfrey laid low after his initial accusations and because he was a serving magistrate, I decided to complain to the Lord Chancellor's Advisory Committee, who oversees magistrates for Hertfordshire, about Mr Palfrey's false accusations. It took them two years to address my complaint. Sir John Brigstocke KCB partially upheld the complaint and considered the length of time taken to deal with it amounted to maladministration. However, Sir John stated that if I decided to take court action against Mr Palfrey and the court concluded that his statement was indeed false then the Advisory Committee would consider Palfrey's suitability to remain as a magistrate.

Even if I proved in court that Palfrey did lie, the Advisory Committee would only consider dismissal and not actively remove him. So I took it no further and decided to leave Palfrey to soak in his mire of lies and concentrate instead on clearing my name against the police allegations.

20 January 2005

STATEMENT OF
P W PALFREY

In February or March 2001, my sister (Mrs Elizabeth M Keenan) told me she, with her daughter, intended to move to a new house in Hemel Hempstead and that her then Partner (Mr Peter J Mahon) would live with them. After the usual problems involved in house buying she decided on a property at ▉▉ ▉▉▉▉▉▉▉▉▉▉ Initially, under persuasion from Mr Mahon, she went through the motions of a joint mortgage application to give him the opportunity to realise his property assets in London, which he said he had, to finance the purchase. It became quickly apparent that he could not, or would not, produce any capital for the purchase. It was at this point my sister asked me for advice as to how to proceed as she had become very apprehensive about the venture. In mid-April she took a determined and intent decision to abandon the initial mortgage enquiry and start afresh by securing a mortgage funded solely by her (and in her name only) to supplement her sole capital investment.

The discussions with, and my advice to, my sister focused on Mr Mahon's financial standing and liabilities. Mr Mahon was plainly a man in his mid to late fifties who had no equity and admitted to no savings with which he could make a contribution to the deposit. His earnings were based on irregular and unreliable sources and could not be relied on to finance mortgage repayments. It appeared to me that his tax and national insurance contributions were suspect and his answer to my sister's question as to "what he would do if the authorities sought anything owed" that he would leave the country, made me apprehensive. Furthermore, his intention to sublease his property in London against the terms of his lease was dubious, especially as the Freeholder – Peabody – being a Charitable Trust would probably be compelled to seek redress for any monies Mr Mahon received from his tenants if he made a profit out of it.

My advice to my sister was that entertaining the purchase of a house with someone like Mr Mahon who had no sense of finance rectitude, or financial stability, was too risky. Furthermore, if she could only rely on herself to fund the mortgage she should do so on the express understanding that the Deeds would be in her name only and she would be solely responsible for the mortgage. Additionally, if Mr Mahon was in any way connected to the property (ie, it could be seen as partly his asset) she would have difficulties if the Inland Revenue or Peabody Trust obtained liability orders against him and wished to exercise them against the house – especially if they were pursing him for money and he had followed through his intention to leave the country and was, therefore, no longer available to them.

1.   'Incredible amount of accusations that could never be proven just to blacken my name which exposes the fact that Palfrey was the instigator behind Liz's false allegations.'

◇◇◇◇◇

CHAPTER 6

To Move Or Not To Move, That Is The Question

It was October 1998 when I first met Liz in a pub at Finsbury Park. It was a place where I had performed many times singing and playing guitar with a four-piece band called the Happy Murphys. On stage we mucked about and joked while we played our version of up-tempo Irish songs. The audiences, mainly drunken Irishmen, argued and threw punches and kicked the bollocks out of each other while we happily ignored them and played our music.

It was Liz's friend Cathy who had persuaded her to go and see the band. When I went over and chatted to them, Cathy did most of the talking. She complained that the pub was rough but it had a better atmosphere than where they lived. When Cathy told me they came from Hemel Hempstead she went into hysterical laughter. She did laugh a lot while Liz just smiled. When I asked her what was so funny about Hemel Hempstead she started laughing again, screaming that the town was so boring you could fall asleep while walking around shopping. I was really enjoying Cathy's humour and although Liz stayed silent most of the time I thought she was very attractive. Liz was a tall well-built woman who appeared sophisticated but she had a mysterious air about her that my inquisitive nature wanted to solve. She seemed shy but confident. We started going out and every time we met she always welcomed me with a big smile and a kiss. She looked so attractive when she smiled that I found it hard to resist her.

That Christmas of 1998, Liz invited me to her house for a Boxing Day meal and to meet her family. I arrived around mid-day to a grand welcome and a meal fit for a king. Her mother was a jolly woman, cuddly and sweet. She told jokes, laughed heartily and constantly criticised

'Him'. It took me a while to realise it was Liz's ex-husband, Steve, who she was talking about and not Scottish Dave, the bloke that Liz had just finished a relationship with. Her mother would continually say 'he was a liar', 'he was a pratt' and 'he was stupid'. I wondered why she was so upset about Liz's ex-husband while Liz appeared not to be particularly bothered.

Liz had also told me a lot about Scottish Dave and said he was still phoning her so I felt there was a strong possibility that she would start seeing him again.

My first impression of Liz's brother Peter Palfrey was that he seemed odd. When he smiled his face looked like a wasp had stung it and his milk of human kindness had certainly turned sour that day we met. He appeared cold and calculating on the exterior but when I got to know him better I realised that inside he was indeed, cold and calculating. He was a serving magistrate at Hemel Hempstead Courts and enjoyed boasting about the stern punishment he dealt out when he was on the bench. He even invited me and Liz to come to the courts to watch him 'perform'. It's a day I want to forget. It was like going into a cupboard to watch paint dry. He took himself very seriously and continually preached to his family about honesty but I was later to find out to my detriment that he really practiced skullduggery. His favourite saying was, "and your point is?" whenever someone was trying to explain something. A conversation with Palfrey was like playing a board game. He always wanted the upper hand.

As Boxing Day came to a close and everyone was leaving to go home Palfrey quietly approached me. "Can I have a private word with you?" he whispered.

I became intrigued. As he spoke in his serious 'Godfather' like voice I wondered what information he would be sharing. Maybe he was going to tell me some ghastly family secret or disclose the fact that he was responsible for England's victory of the Second World War. But no, he wanted to warn me about going out with his sister and told me she was still recovering from her previous boyfriend, Scottish Dave. He, of course told me that this conversation was for my benefit only and felt he was duty bound to advise me not to get involved with his sister, Liz.

I looked at him and thought, "is this guy on drugs! What sort of an eejit does he take me for? I can make my own decision without having to refer to the family know-it-all". I decided to be polite and say nothing. It was hard to keep my mouth shut but I swallowed my opinion and listened. I told him I already knew about Liz's previous relationship with Scottish Dave because Liz had told me. He stressed again that he was only telling me this for my own good. "I bet you are," I thought. I didn't dare mention this to Liz.

In the summer of 2000, I received a letter from the freeholders of the flat where I lived stating that there was the possibility that the whole block would be demolished. I had bought the lease of my shop and three-bedroom flat in 1988 and was not intending to move. When I told Liz about the possible demolition, that's when she suggested I should live with her. At first I said no, I didn't want to move to Hemel

Hempstead. I liked where I lived and even though I liked being wildly in love with Liz, Hemel was not a town I even considered moving to. The thought of living together was very appealing but living with Liz in London was more appealing than living in Hemel.

As the months went by it was starting to look more and more possible that I would have to sell or become homeless. Liz once again suggested that we should live together but I was very reluctant to move out of London. She didn't want to move out of Hemel so I had to decide what to do. I talked it over with some of my friends and they all agreed that Liz was really nice and this confirmed to me that I was making the right decision. So I decided to move to Hemel Hempstead.

Liz suggested we buy a house together and I thought it was a great idea. We went around estate agents and finally found a house we both liked that also had potential for extending and improving. It was March 2001 when we sat down with a mortgage lender and signed a joint application. I agreed with Liz that she should handle the financial side of things and I would take charge of the decorating and building work.

Three months passed and still not a word about how much my contribution would have to be for the deposit. Then in June 2001, Liz suddenly told me there had been a change to the mortgage arrangements. She said her brother, Palfrey, had advised her to get a mortgage on her own. He told her it would be more secure for her to exclude me as she was paying the majority of the deposit. I had to agree. She said her brother had reminded her that 'with her track record with men, she would be better off getting a mortgage on her own.' Her brother must have had a very low opinion of Liz's choice of partners and of course he had included me in this list. I considered pulling out but my love was too strong and so I agreed to continue with the purchase on her terms. She did need my monetary help with the mortgage payments and so I agreed to move in with her even though I had no security. What can I say? I was in love.

"You'll be in my will and if anything unfortunate should happen to me, then my brother who will be executor of my affairs, will make sure you get your share," claimed Liz.

It all sounded very simple. We discussed it for an hour or so and I was slowly becoming persuaded to the idea but I was still not convinced about the financial set-up. As we talked, Liz kept looking at her watch and then she announced that she had a meeting to go to with her solicitor and would I come along? I said, "There was no point". I didn't understand why she wanted me to come, especially as I was now no longer included in the purchase of the house. But she insisted I come with her for support. She eventually persuaded me and I reluctantly went with her to her solicitors. We arrived at his office where I expected to sit and watch her sign some papers confirming that the house is now just a solo project. But to my surprise the solicitor slid a form across the desk for me to sign.

"Why have I to sign?" I asked.

"It is a form of consent," said the solicitor casually. "It's to prevent you having any claim on the property if it should go into receivership."

I looked over at Liz. She had a look of panic on her face. I was confused. Why should I sign this? I'm not on the mortgage and maybe I shouldn't even be living there. Liz said nothing. The solicitor just sat there looking at us. I didn't want to start an argument there and then so I sat like a dummy, motionless and stupefied. I had been persuaded to go to this meeting and now I was put in the awkward position of signing something I didn't want to sign. I looked at Liz again. I looked at the solicitor. Not a word was said and then like a fool I grabbed the form and signed it. I was raging inside and fuming at having to sign this agreement under pressure. I didn't even read it. We went out of the office and into the street. My stomach was tightening into knots.

"What the hell is going on?" I snapped. "Did you know this was going to happen?"

"No."

"Is that why you asked me to come with you?"

"Of course not!" She said.

Liz was not happy at my reaction. She drove us back to her house and all through the journey I just sat in the car wondering what to do. We went into the house and continued to argue. I was very angry and was now definitely not going to be any part of this new house. I would not move to Hemel. Liz got angry and continually denied having any advanced knowledge about the form of consent I had signed. She just repeated that it was still going to be 'our home'.

After a few minutes arguing I told her that I wanted nothing to do with the purchase and would be staying in London. Even though I loved Liz I was unwilling to get involved in something that could leave me financially vulnerable. Liz started crying. I offered her the choice to come and live with me but she didn't want to do that because of her daughter, Laura, and her job. We cuddled and kissed and she pleaded with me to move in with her. She slowly persuaded me that it would be for the best if we lived together in Hemel Hempstead and I could rent out my flat in London for extra income. Then we went to bed. I allowed my heart to overrule my head.

When we talked about my move, we agreed that I would pay for all the improvements and half of everything else. That would be my contribution until I sold my flat or received compensation for its demolition and then that money would go towards our home and make us equal partners. It all seemed logical at the time and I was persuaded that it was for the best so we could stay together.

There were a few hiccups with exchange of contracts but eventually in August 2001 we moved into 18 Adeyfield Gardens, Hemel Hempstead. That first night I felt a bit uncomfortable and doubts were nagging me that I may have made a mistake. To agree to a partnership without some written guarantee was not the smartest move I had ever made but I convinced myself that I was only imagining things and this was just a glitch. I was at the beginning of a love story that would last forever. Who cares about money when you are in love?

I discovered years later, after my eviction, that she had changed the mortgage agreement four days after we had signed a joint mortgage and did not tell me of this new arrangement until that day, three months later when we went to her solicitor's office. I also discovered that she had opened a letter addressed to me from the mortgage company, kept it hidden from me and replied on my behalf claiming I had consulted with an independent solicitor, which I hadn't, about the new arrangements. There had also been a shortfall of £8000 that initially I would have paid but without my knowledge her brother Palfrey paid the money. Finding out all this after four years showed me that the relationship had been built on deceit. Liz and her brother had set me up from day one. I was devastated and felt betrayed.

As well as moving to Hemel in 2001 it was the year my father died. He quietly passed away in his sleep at 7.20am on 7 September in Belfast City Hospital. I was on the upper deck of a London bus when my sister rang to tell me the sad news. Even though we had never been very close, I stared out the window regretting I hadn't been there to say goodbye to him. Now it was too late. I always wanted to talk to my dad about the many things I never understood about my childhood. Why, for example, had I been brought up by my Aunt and not by him? The chance is now gone. Thank God he's not around to see the mess I've got myself into. Liz, Caolan, Jenna and I went to Belfast for the funeral and Liz was very supportive to me through those sad days. We flew back to London on the same day, and at the same time, the two planes flew into the Twins Towers in New York.

I look back on why I moved to Hemel Hempstead and wonder how I survived the boring night life in that small town compared to the exciting and manic bright lights of London. Love was the reason, or so I told myself and Liz was the reason I loved Hemel. But I didn't love Hemel, it was Liz that I loved and she was the reason I moved there.

CHAPTER 7

⟨⟩⟨⟩⟨⟩⟨⟩⟨⟩

"I Want You Out"

I didn't fit into a routine for quite some time the first year I lived at Adeyfield Gardens and I was missing my friends, family and the excitement of the concrete jungle of London. Hemel is a small town and a small town can be a shock to the system after a big city. If it hadn't have been for the neighbours on each side of us, who were both called John, I would have felt lonely and abandoned during daylight hours while Liz was at work.

Being a musician, most of my work was at week-ends leaving my week days free to go to acting auditions and rehearse my music. John at number 16 invited me into his kitchen nearly every morning for a coffee and a gossip about the happenings in our street and John at number 20 chatted with me in the back garden while we enjoyed afternoon tea and his wife's home-made cakes. I was living the suburban good life with the two Johns.

In 2001, Liz and I got stuck into doing work on the house and I took on the impossible task of building a walk-in wardrobe in Laura's bedroom. I had never done anything as daring as this before and when it was finished Laura and Liz loved it. Liz showed it off to her friends and family who all thought it was marvellous and of course this encouraged me to move onto bigger and more adventurous jobs.

I painted everywhere, stripped all the wood on the banisters, which took forever, laid a new wooden floor in the hall, fitted new spotlights in the hall and bathroom, changed the interior doors and front door and took on the horrendous job of moving the front garden to the back of the house. I was planning to build a patio at the front of the house to park our two cars on. I spent weeks landscaping the tons of soil piled at the back of the house that appeared to be a 100 feet high. I had never worked so hard in such a long time and my back was killing me. Liz stood staring out of the kitchen window as I shovelled and racked for weeks to try to landscape the back garden. When I finished I stumbled into the kitchen covered in mud, crippled with backache and exhausted from the physical nightmare of digging a garden that seemed to stretch for miles. She stood motionless, glaring at this bedraggled tramp that appeared to have just stepped out of a swamp. I was hoping she would feel sorry for me but there was no reaction.

From 2001 to 2003 the relationship appeared to be perfect. I was happy and all my friends and family thought I had met the perfect partner. Having gone out with girls of every size, shape and predicament, Liz was the sexy, intelligent woman I had been hoping for. I was besotted with her and I thought she was madly in love with me. Even though we appeared financially comfortable with earnings from our respective careers, Liz never disclosed how much she earned. I sometimes wondered why she never told me because most couples would share this information, especially when setting up home together. But if she wanted to keep her earnings secret I didn't care. I still felt I was the luckiest man in Hemel Hempstead with the most amazing woman in the county of Hertfordshire.

When I bought a Celtic diamond ring for Liz, to show her my eternal love and also to demonstrate a public gesture that we would eventually get married; her family were excited except for her brother, Palfrey. He asked Liz to take the ring off and then began examining the inside looking for the hallmark. I sat there watching him and thinking to myself, "he must be trying to work out how much it cost". Liz and her sister and mother didn't notice; they were too busy laughing and chatting in the corner of the room. I waited for his expert opinion of the value but he said nothing. He just looked at me very strangely. No one else in the room seemed to notice his behaviour but I was bemused as to why he appeared so annoyed. As the years went by I started to realise that there were three people in our relationship and I was the one being slowly pushed out of the metaphorical bed. Palfrey's sarcastic comments from time to time confirmed to me that this man had a problem with me being involved with his sister.

Throughout 2003 Liz seemed to be getting more stressed at work. She had been at Grovehill Medical Centre long before I had met her. Doctor Hirji was the senior partner and liked Liz a lot because she was good at her job and excelled in everything she did. When the job of Practice Manager became vacant it was Liz who was the obvious choice to take the position.

It was soon after she took the job that things started to change. She would come home exhausted and sometimes crying. She was finding it too demanding because of the pressure of learning so much in such a short space of time. I tried to encourage her and would often comfort her when she needed a cuddle or two. She was starting to get depressed and when I asked her if she was okay, she always put it down to stress at work and 'women's problems'. She thought she was going through the change of life for as she was now in her mid-40s. I kept telling her to see her own doctor to find out what the problem was but she just refused to talk about it. I threw myself into the refurbishment of our home and that helped me cope with Liz's depression. I also took a part time job as a driver in July 2004 so we could save extra money for the big family trip to America I was planning.

Liz was becoming more distant and didn't appear to be interested in going places with me anymore. When she went shopping she couldn't care less if I came along or not, whereas before she would always insist that I go too. In the bedroom she was cold as ice, refusing to have sex with me. Then one day in September 2004 I eventually challenged her in the kitchen about her behaviour.

"Liz, why are you so cold towards me these days, is there something wrong?"

She stopped and turned and just for a couple of seconds, hesitated and then blurted:

"It's over, I want you out."

I stood there in astonishment and my first thought was she must have met someone else. She denied being involved with another man and said she just wanted to finish our relationship. Apparently she had been considering it for some time but added that she still wanted us to remain friends. That's when she gave me a friendly smile. I was puzzled at her behaviour because I hadn't suspected anything. I knew she was depressed but I believed her when she told me it was the pressure of work and nothing else. I suggested we try and work things out but she insisted that she wanted us to finish. Then she announced that one of the reasons was that I really didn't get on with her family. I was flabbergasted. I had thought that taking her mother shopping every week and driving her sister to her regular hospital appointments in London showed there was no friction between her family and me. But then she said it was her brother I didn't get on with. It was true that I thought he was someone who couldn't be trusted but I had always restrained myself from having any confrontations with him.

"Anyway, what's your brother got to do with us?"

She didn't answer and just repeated that she had decided she wanted me out. I reluctantly agreed and said I would be out by Christmas if I could arrange some alternative accommodation. I then reminded her of the money I had put towards the improvements of our home. She said I would get that money back but that was the moment I noticed the friendly smile drop from her face. I felt hurt inside and confused. Of course I was angry at losing my lover but restoring the armour I had built around myself and determined not to let emotion take control, I sat motionless. I hadn't seen this coming. Why was she rejecting me without a reasonable excuse? I could feel the hurt inside eating me up. I sat silent, trying to think of something to say that would change her mind. Then I broke down.

"This is not right," I said, "I've given up everything for you and now you're tossing me aside like an old... potted plant"

She stood staring at me with a look of distaste.

"This is not fair!" I shouted.

She turned and walked out of the kitchen.

The next few days we hardly spoke to each other and when I tried to have a conversation she just blanked me. We continued sleeping in the same bed but in a strange atmosphere between us with no sign of affection. There wasn't much room in the bed with her, the metaphorical elephant and me. Then she told me that her brother had advised her not to give me back a penny of the money I had contributed towards our home. I was to leave before Christmas with nothing.

The silence continued and every time I walked into a room she walked out. We ate separately even though I still tried to continue with a normal routine. Laura didn't speak much either and kept herself to herself in her room. It was a very uncomfortable situation. Liz watched TV in the living room, I watched TV in the kitchen. I decided to go to my solicitor in London to ask him what he considered to be my best course of action. He suggested that he could write a letter to her and point out that I am entitled to a beneficial interest in the house. I suggested moving out until the matter was settled but he told me under no circumstances should I leave.

He said it could affect my claim so I had to put up with the uncomfortable atmosphere of living in a house where I was ignored. I didn't really know what to do and possibly a room at Battersea Dogs Home would be a better choice than living in the 'house of silence'. I found out, after I had been evicted, that leaving my home would not have affected my beneficial claim. If only I had known that before I took my solicitors advice, then things would have been a whole lot different. When Liz received my solicitor's letter informing her that I would not be moving out until some kind of financial agreement had been made, she left bedclothes on the sofa demanding I sleep in the living room. I didn't expect that. I still got up before Liz in the morning, got my clothes from the bedroom, had my breakfast and woke her before I went to work but I did stop bringing her breakfast in bed. I thought about continuing this ritual but then on second thoughts, she might throw it back at me. She had become very volatile and any 'of the cuff' remark might trigger a full-blown argument.

"Why don't we sit down and talk about this, Liz," I suggested again.

"No! I want you out," she snapped.

I felt so down. Friends and neighbours were starting to notice my sad demeanour. My daughter Jenna asked me what was wrong because like everyone else she had sensed unhappiness in the air. I reluctantly told her that Liz wanted us to break up. So Jenna phoned Liz to find out what was going on. Liz told her that she was just feeling down and even though it wasn't my fault, she still wanted to finish with me. Nothing was making sense. I tried to unearth why Liz was behaving negatively towards me but all I got was, 'I want you out'.

"Look Liz, I don't want the house or a share of it, I just want the money I put into our home."

"You put nothing into my house," she shouted, "and if you don't leave I'll report you to the taxman."

I froze for a second. I just couldn't believe what she had just said. She knew I paid tax because she had helped me with my accounts and together we always worked through my tax returns. Why was she threatening me with that? The look on her face told me she meant it.

By following my solicitor's advice, I thought she might have begun to see reason and that was why I agreed to wait and hope for an amicable outcome. But Liz didn't budge; she got really infuriated and went straight off to tell her brother, Palfrey, about my solicitor's letter. He came up with, as he thought, the brilliant idea of going to the Domestic Violence unit at Hemel police station and telling them that she felt threatened. 'Mr Mahon's demand for money is tantamount to psychological abuse,' Palfrey later wrote in his statement to the police. That was something I never expected Liz to agree with.

Unbeknown to me, Liz and Palfrey had gone to Hemel police station on 14 December 2004 and requested that I be removed from my home on 19 December. Neither the police or Palfrey and Liz considered this to be illegal.

I arrived home on the 17 December and found a letter[1] on the kitchen table addressed to me. It stated, *my solicitor has written to your solicitor and made our position clear. I must therefore inform you that I have spoken to the police regarding the situation of you being given notice to leave on Sunday and they said that*

1

regardless of what the solicitors say, they will come and remove you from the premises if you do not go willingly.

I went straight into the living room where Liz and Laura were sitting watching television. I asked her why she had written the letter and she said her brother had advised her to do so.

I pointed out that solicitors were already involved so why would she get the police. "You won't leave so the police will kick you out," she said. I told her it would be a better idea to get proper advice because the police wouldn't be interested in a minor civil dispute like this. And that's what I thought.

 "My brother gives me all the advice I need and the police said they will remove you!"

I thought she was bluffing so I turned and walked out of the room.

Liz avoided me for the next two days and I was left alone in the house all day Saturday and Sunday. It didn't seem real the way Liz was behaving and it had me totally perplexed. I just couldn't concentrate properly on anything.

On the morning of that Sunday 19 December 2004, I was suddenly woken by the loud bang of the front door closing at around 8am. This was very unusual because Liz loved to have a lie in on Sundays and have breakfast in bed. I climbed out of the sofa bed and looked around the house. Both Liz and Laura were gone. This was very strange, but it was only four days to Christmas so maybe they had gone on a big shopping trip. I hung around the house all morning until lunchtime and still there was no sign of them. I considered going to her mother's to see if she was there but I changed my mind and just decided to wait in the house. But they never returned. So that evening I went and did my gig in London as usual.

I arrived home around midnight and unloaded my equipment. I went to the bathroom and could hear the television was on in Liz's bedroom but I decided not to say anything. As I crawled into my make-shift bed I heard a phone ring upstairs and that's when I noticed the living room phone was missing. "That's strange..." but then I didn't give it another thought. As I laid my head on the pillow I heard someone upstairs dialling out. Maybe Laura was out somewhere and Liz was waiting for her safe return. I was asleep in seconds only to be woken by the sight of two uniformed officers. Had Liz booked two gay strip-o-grams as a surprise for Christmas? No, they were two police officers booked for a surprise eviction.

(CJ Act 1967 s.9; MC Act 1980 ss.5A, (3) (s) and 5B, MC Rules 1981 r.70)

URN				

Statement of   Elizabeth Keenan

Age if under 18   over 18   (if over 18 insert "over 18")   Occupation   Practice Manager

This statement (consisting of 5 pages each signed by me) is true to the best of my knowledge and belief and I make it knowing that, if it is tendered in evidence, I shall be liable to prosecution if I have wilfully stated in it anything which I know to be false or do not believe to be true.

Signature   *EnKeena*   Date 21/02/06

Tick if witness evidence is visually recorded [ ] (supply witness details)

This statement is in relation to a complaint made by Mr Peter Mahon about officer's Hughes 2044, Thurston 1222 and O Neill 500 involvement in dealing with a domestic incident, where by Mr Mahon alleges he was evicted on the 20th December 2004, from ~~████████████~~ Hemel Hempstead.

On Friday 17th December 04, due to fear I could not speak to Mr Mahon about my visit to the police, so I gave him a letter to inform him of it. In the letter I quoted the advice from the police which was, regardless of what solicitors said they could come and remove Mr Mahon because of the circumstances and his behaviour I had described to them. Although the police did not actually use these exact words, this was the impression I gained. In the letter I also informed Mr Mahon of my deep distress and that

My Solicitor has written to your Solicitor and made our position clear.

I must, therefore, inform you that I have spoken to the Police regarding the situation of you being given notice to leave the premises on Sunday and they have said that, regardless of what the solicitors say, they will come and remove you from the premises if you do not go willingly.

I am sorry that it has come to this but the only way I can try and cope with the situation is not to speak to you at this time and look after the needs of my daughter as best I possibly can.

Yours sincerely

Liz

LIZ KEENAN
17th DECEMBER 2004

2.   'First letter from Liz claiming police stated I would be evicted by them and her contradicting witness statement made one year later admitting the police did not state they would evict me.'

CHAPTER 8

◇◇◇◇◇

Tattoo

The two tenants in my east London flat were very obliging when I told them I was homeless and so they offered to move out before their tenancy agreement had ended. I moved back in at the beginning of February 2005 and just sat in front of the portable television that my daughter had given me. Liz and I had four televisions in our home in Hemel, two of which I had bought but she kept them all. I watched the video 'In the name of the father' over and over again and when the judge sentenced Gerry Conlon, who was played by Daniel Day-Lewis, to a lifetime behind bars, I felt anger. My insides cringed and tears filled my eyes witnessing the injustice that was being dealt out because of corrupt police officers that had lied. Of course the injustice was of a completely different magnitude to mine but it was still down to the lying arm of the law and that's what was causing me to cry.

I felt depressed. I was losing weight, couldn't sleep and started having flashbacks to the eviction. I just sat around feeling down and drinking more often than I had ever drunk before. I was never a big drinker but now I was doing it every night. I phoned friends, I phoned ex-girlfriends, I phoned anyone who would listen to my drunken slobbering. I even phoned the Samaritans one night and though the man I spoke to was as helpful as a toothbrush to a budgie, I was so glad to talk to someone. I appreciate that they do help many other people in distress, but not me. Maybe my case was too complicated for the public to understand but I became obsessed with telling people about the injustice I had received. Anyone who had the patience to listen to me just stared. Distressed and despairing I talked and talked while they all wore the same expression on their faces, HELP! Talking was a form of therapy for me I suppose and it was free, except I had to buy the drinks most of the time. I joined in on conversations in pubs with total strangers and always found a way to shift the conversation round to my problem. "That was a depressing evening," I overheard one woman say. "I'm never coming back to this pub again."

My friend Jim Bradford recommended that I meet up with a friend of his wife, Simon Groom, who was going through a similar situation. Simon was suing the police for false arrest and false allegations. He was one step ahead of me in the legal process because his case had started long before mine. I was able to copy procedures that he had already established and achieved because I no longer had a solicitor helping me. My solicitor, Mr Roberts, had suggested I deal with the police myself to save money while he continued representing me with my beneficial claim against Liz. Simon helped by telling me which forms to fill in and I followed his advice to the letter until he reached the High Court and lost his Judicial Review appeal. That's when I was out on my own venturing into the unknown realm of legal territory. Somewhere I'd never been before.

Jim also advised me to speak to another friend, Maurice McElroy, who had some knowledge of legal matters. I needed his help on how to make a complaint about the police officers. I was just getting nowhere with my letters of complaint and phone calls. We sat down at his computer and he wrote a letter to Professional Standards complaining about the actions of the two officers.

I was now in such a state that I could hardly string two words together let alone write another letter of complaint. The trouble with shock is that it is not always evident to the naked eye but Maurice said he knew me well enough to see that I was seriously disturbed.

I visited my doctor that month as the whole affair was getting me down so much I felt drained and confused. But the truth was not so obvious. He prescribed anti-depressants and advised me to seek some kind of therapy.

I know Americans constantly talk about their therapists like we talk about our relatives but back in the wilderness of a small town like Downpatrick, outside Belfast, the stigma of having a mental illness would sow doubts among friends and neighbours about my sanity. The word psychiatric was not commonly used in my part of Northern Ireland because most of us didn't know what it meant. I grew up thinking that people '*like that*' go to a hospital called 'The Mental'. So with a childhood memory that anyone who was depressed should be locked up, I was not prepared to admit that I needed help.

A friend of mine, Steve Latner, dragged me out to his photography group once a week in the hope it would help me forget my problems. The group overwhelmingly supported me in my troubles and I felt like I had joined a religious cult that was praying for my safe return to normality. I also had my old musician friend, Gerry Tweedie phoning me every week from Ireland to offer his support and advice. So I hadn't been totally abandoned.

I eventually received a reply from Hertfordshire's Professional Standards stating that my complaint had been recorded as a 'Direction and

Control' issue. What the hell that meant I didn't have a clue but I think it means 'we don't give a bugger about your complaint'. They promised to report back when the matter had been looked into. But I continued writing, sending evidence and phoning various officers who were supposed to be in charge of the matter until July 2005, when the police informed me that they now considered my complaint so serious it should be handed over to their Legal Services Department. The Legal Services solicitor, Mrs Grundy, continued corresponding with me for months though she avoided answering questions and refused to release statements that were accusing me of 'whatever'. She just wouldn't tell me what I had been accused of.

Then an Inspector Mutum from Hertfordshire Constabulary offered me an interview with the two officers, at a fee of £85 per officer! They said it would help clear up the matter and bring it to a close. At £85 per officer I would expect a meal with a live band and a good bottle of wine and that was never going to happen. I agreed to the meeting but then Mrs Grundy withdrew the offer and refused any further contact, saying the matter was now closed. She stated: '*The investigation into your claim of unlawful eviction has been concluded and there is no requirement for you to be interviewed*'. She refused to take statements from anyone and yet claimed that she had done a thorough investigation. In her words: '*The officers had used common law powers to remove you from the property.*' But I was to discover from three senior police officers that the two coppers had exceeded their 'common law powers.' Mrs Grundy was now misquoting the law or lying.

HERTFORDSHIRE
CONSTABULARY

RFB Solicitors

London

Date:	1ˢᵗ July 2005
Our Ref:	Mahon
Your Ref:	JAR/LV/M118.2
Contact:	Mrs A Grundy
Direct Line:	
Direct Fax:	
E-mail:	

Dear Sirs,

On the 1ˢᵗ March 2005 your client wrote to the Head of the Professional Standards Office setting out his complaint and alleging that PC Thurston and PC Hughes had acted unlawfully.

Your client's complaint was recorded as a 'Direction and Control' issue and referred to the relevant Area for investigation. Inspector Paul Mutum and C/Superintendent Chris Taylor explained to yourselves and Tony McWalter MP that your client had not been evicted from the premises and had acted lawfully.

Your client was obviously unhappy with the explanation given as you then wrote to PC Thurston directly on the 5ᵗʰ April 2005 seeking an interview. It was at that time that Legal Services were made aware of this matter and sought a full explanation of your client's allegations.

We have reviewed the Police logs known as URN's and the crime report. There is a Common Law power available to the officers to prevent a breach of the peace and it was this power the officers were relying upon when they asked your client to vacate the above property.

In light of our review we are satisfied that the officers acted lawfully on the 20ᵗʰ December 2005 and liability is denied. It is denied that your client's complaint has not been progressed satisfactorily or that we have been obstructive.

We have advised the officers concerned that they do not have to agree to your requests to interview them. If your client wishes to pursue this matter further then we are instructed to act on behalf of the Chief Constable of the Hertfordshire Constabulary and can accept service of proceedings on his behalf.

Yours faithfully

Mrs Allison Grundy
Solicitor, Legal Services

Encs.

cc. Mr. Peter Mahon,

3.   'Letter from Grundy (police solicitor) contradicting Chief Supt Taylor's letter.'

HERTFORDSHIRE
CONSTABULARY

Mr. Peter Mahon

Date:	6th July 2005
Our Ref:	Mahon
Your Ref:	
Contact:	Mrs A Grundy
Direct Line:	01707 354175
Direct Fax:	01707 354518
E-mail:	

Dear Sir,

Re: ████████████ Hemel Hempstead

Thank you for your letter dated 4th July 2005.

The investigation into your claim of unlawful eviction has been concluded and there is no requirement for you to be interviewed. Liability has been denied on behalf of the Chief Constable and we have advised that the police officers concerned do not have to submit to interview by you or your solicitor.

It is not usual for officers to be interviewed by a claimant when allegations of this nature have been made.

If you wish to pursue the matter further then you should take independent legal advice on making a claim through the County Court against the Chief Constable.

We are unable to advise you regarding the forthcoming Beneficial Interest Case at Watford County Court in August 2005 and you should seek advice from your own solicitor regarding this matter.

Yours faithfully

Mrs Allison Grundy
Solicitor, Legal Services

- 2 33 -

Legal Services
Police Headquarters, Stanborough Road, Welwyn Garden City, Herts AL8 6XF

4.   'One of Grundy's attempts to cover-up unlawful eviction.'

Things just dragged on but God bless the internet, I found a support group called 'False Allegations Support Organisation' and I phoned them. They were very helpful and advised me to contact the Independent Police Complaints Commission (IPCC), which at that time I had never heard of. So I wrote a letter and to my surprise the IPCC informed me that my complaint to the police had not even been recorded. I couldn't believe it, after six months of complaining I now had to make a complaint about the non-recording of my complaint. Another three months dragged on and the IPCC eventually upheld my complaint and instructed the police to investigate. Professional Standards would handle the investigation and I was now convinced my name would be cleared. I got really excited but then I was warned by a writer friend, Leslie Naylor, who wrote a book about miscarriages of justice called *Judge for Yourself*, that an investigation into the police by Professional Standards is like the Third Reich investigating the SS for war crimes. Surely that can't be true? I was still naive enough to think that corruption within the police would easily be exposed. But dark clouds were starting to appear. The more I complained to the authorities the more I ended up in blind alleys. I was sent round in circles to only arrive where I had started.

I spent the summer of 2005 writing letters and statements, phoning solicitors, visiting every Law Centre and every Citizens Advice Bureau I could find to get help. But as soon as I mentioned suing the police, nobody wanted to know. One solicitor slammed the phone down on me, another told me, "I had a good case but didn't have a hope in hell of winning" and another told me, "if I had plenty of money then I might win". Everyone appeared to be frightened to take on the police and I was branded a fool or even worse, crazy for trying. My cousin Clare, who is notorious for being a fighter against injustice, also told me not to bother and to walk away. There was one glimmer of hope though when a solicitor told me that I might have a good claim for infringement of my human rights. But I only had one year to make a claim and then she told me she was too busy to take on my case.

I just spent every day staring at my computer screen until I collapsed. I was slowly going mad. Builders had started renovating the block of flats where I lived so I couldn't hear conversations on the phone properly and the noise of constant drilling even drowned out my thoughts. The freeholders had changed their mind and decided not to demolish my block of flats but refurbish them instead. This noise continued for over a year and then things got worse. A squatter, who happened to be a musician, moved into the flat directly above my bedroom and started playing his saxophone every night from 3am. I had drilling by day and sax by night. I was exhausted. I just wasn't getting any peace or sleep. I asked him politely to play at a reasonable time of the day but he continued playing every night. I complained to the council, the noise nuisance authorities, the housing association and even the police but no one was willing to help. All the neighbours were screaming at him but yet he continued. So after months of this torture I went to his front door and banged on it really hard.

"Hey man, what's your problem?" he shouted, standing in his underwear in a drug-induced state.

I politely tried to explain that playing a saxophone at 3am was disturbing everyone's sleep in the block.

"Go and have some sex, man!" he laughed and started closing the door.

"Don't close the door on me while I'm talking!" I shouted.

"Fuck off!" he said.

I stuck my foot in front of the door and then pushed it open. He stepped back in surprise. I noticed out of the corner of my eye the fuse board above the doorway and because I'm tall I was able to reach it and switch off the electricity supply. I then began to remove all the fuses. I turned and walked away with his only means of electricity power in my hands. He begged me for hours to return them, banging on my door, shouting through my window.

"Hey man, I have no heating, no lighting. I can't have a shower. I need my fuses."

"Piss off squatter!" I shouted.

He eventually moved out after being forced to sit in candlelight for two days.

I had locked myself away in my flat for months. I knew I had to get out, back into reality, so I went down Brick Lane to sit in the sunlight and drink coffee while watching the world go by. It did help and the sun on my face reminded me of happier times. I looked at every woman that resembled Liz. Having considered Liz to have been the most genuine person I had ever known, I was now deeply confused whom I could trust. It had taken nearly a year for me to realise that Liz must have been the sincerest liar I had ever met. I also noticed that a lot of women in Brick Lane had tattoos of one kind or another. It was a trend that seemed to be getting more and more popular. This also reminded me of Liz. She always wanted to get a tattoo. I didn't really care for them at that time but in my present state of mind, I felt the time was now right to make a gesture of disgust against Liz and get a tattoo.

I paced up and down outside the tattoo shop in Shoreditch trying to build up the courage to go inside. Eventually I went in. A big tattooed American guy asked if I needed some help. He offered me a collection of books with numerous photos of bodies covered in various symbols and designs. I looked through the pages while I listened to some poor sod screaming in the next room as the drill whined away like the sound you hear in a dentist's surgery. Now was my chance to get out of there before I made a mistake or go into what sounded like a torture chamber. But no, I decided to stay and face the consequences. I told the American that I wanted 'this', and handed him a piece of paper with some writing on it. He asked if I had a design in mind so I told him I fancied big Celtic writing. "Where do you want it?" he asked. "On my arse," I replied and I pointed to the left side of my bottom. He asked for a £100 and so I took out my wallet. Unfortunately, I only had £70 in it. He admitted it had been a quiet day so he agreed to do it for this. He took me into a small room and told me to drop my trousers. As I lay face down on his table I started thinking, "What am I doing? Why am I getting a tattoo? It's a solicitor I need not a bloody tattoo."

The sound of the needle started and I gripped tight onto the table expecting horrendous pain. I was right. It was very painful. As the needle pieced my skin I closed my eyes tight and the nightmare of my eviction flashed before me.

"Wake up! Wake up!" shouted Liz.

"If you don't leave the house immediately, I will arrest you!" shouted PC Hughes.

"You can't do that!" I screamed.

"Oh yes I can!" And Hughes's grinning face moved closer and closer to mine.

The needle stopped.

"Are you okay?"

"What?" I opened my eyes. "Yes, fine. Is that it?"

"I don't think so," he laughed, "we've just started."

"Oh."

The drilling resumed and once again I closed my eyes hoping that if I couldn't see then I wouldn't feel. But the nightmare was still very clear and fresh in my thoughts.

"If you don't leave immediately I will arrest you," PC Hughes said with a malicious grin.

Liz stood laughing with a look of evil in her eyes.

"But I haven't done anything!" I pleaded. Hughes laughed and then pushed me out the door.

"Phew! All done," sighed the tattooist.

It was three hours later, the nightmares were over and the tattoo was finished. I got up and stuck my arse in front a mirror. I peered through my legs and then round my sides. "Yes. That's it."

Off I went with the tattoo on my arse and a smile on my face. The experience had lifted my depression momentarily and if I do live to regret it, it's only on a part of my body that not many people will have the displeasure of seeing.

"You got a tattoo on your arse?" hollered my friend Dermot. "You must be going insane!"

Dermot and I would spend hours in Brick Lane coffee shops. We would talk – ostensibly about the police but actually about my life. I had many acquaintances but Dermot was a friend I could speak with such honesty. He now considered me to be obsessed with Liz and her lies. Maybe I was but I wasn't prepared to listen to anyone who didn't agree with my determination to prove my innocence.

I went out that night to meet a couple of friends in the Royal Oak pub in Columbia Road, Steve H and Steve L. Steve H was debating with Steve L whether or not he fancied the tall blonde at the bar but Steve L was adamant that he had a girlfriend and was staying faithful. So Steve H turned to me and asked if I fancied any of the two girls? I told him I didn't fancy anybody and had had enough of women.

"Pull yourself together mate and forget 'bout that fuckin' bitch Liz or whatever her name was," he said, "what you need to do is give that bird over there a good seeing to up the wrong-on'. That will sort you out!"

"What are you talking about?"

"He means a shag up the arse," laughed Steve L.

Then both Steves burst out laughing. I could never understand why the mention of arseholes made the two Steves fall about in hysterics. Every time the word was mentioned they would collapse in side-splitting laughter. I didn't dare tell them I had just got a tattoo on my arse.

One of the two girls, who at Steve H's invitation were now sitting at our table, was Lithuanian; the other was English and looked like that girl with the glasses from the Hi De Hi TV show. The Lithuanian girl's command of the English language was not totally understandable and the Hi De Hi girl was so intoxicated that her drunken slur could have been mistaken for Lithuanian.

When she told me she loved watching movies to learn English she emphasised each word incorrectly.

"Half you saw da fillum *Quiet Sheep?*"

"Never heard of it!" I slurred, "Who was in it?"

"Da men calls… Hannibal."

"I know what she means," piped up Steve L, "*Silence of the Lambs.*"

The night flew by and I don't know how it happened but probably with a combination of too much alcohol and Steve H's wit and good looks, we were escorting these two women to a penthouse apartment some-where off Brick Lane. We partied and danced into the small hours of the morning and then Steve disappeared into another room with Ms Hi De Hi. I was left with the Lithuanian girl and we were slow dancing, slow caressing and then slow kissing.

I unbuttoned her blouse and she loosened my trousers. At that point I felt it was only polite to ask her name. There I was standing with my pants round my feet and we hadn't even been officially introduced. She told me her name was difficult to pronounce so to make things easier I could call her 'Liz'. I nearly collapsed. Of all the names to pick, why that one? I immediately pulled my pants up again because I didn't want her to see what was tattooed on my bum. She may not have realised or even understood but I was not willing to start giving an explanation of why I had '*Liz, you're a lying bitch*' written on my arse.

CHAPTER 9

◇◇◇◇◇

THE TRUTH OF THEIR LIES

HERTFORDSHIRE CONSTABULARY

☎ **Direct Line:** 01923 472081
✉ **E-Mail:** chris.taylor@herts.pnn.police.uk

Ref: CT/LW/02-038
Your Ref: MAHN001/hemel

22nd February 2005

Tony McWalter, MP
House of Commons
London
SW1A 0AA

Dear Tony,

Thank you for your letter dated 8th February 2005 concerning your constituent Peter Mahon. I have reviewed police records in relation to this incident. They indicate that police officers attended ███████████████, Hemel Hempstead on 20th December 2004 and dealt with a domestic violence incident in which it was alleged that Mr Mahon had been verbally aggressive to his partner, Mrs Elizabeth Keenan of the same address.

On police arrival, Mr Mahon continued to be verbally aggressive and was swearing. He was asked to leave by police. Mr Mahon was not evicted from the premises. He was asked to leave in an attempt to resolve an ongoing potentially violent situation. Police Officers do not have powers to formally evict anybody from premises and would need a relevant court order to do so. There is no indication on police records that they were acting in concert with any other agency to obtain the formal eviction of Mr Mahon.

This is a relatively complicated situation and I have therefore tasked Inspector Mutum, my Service Improvement Manager, with fully researching the incident. He will provide you with a more detailed written reply.

Yours sincerely

Chief Supt Chris Taylor
Area Commander
Western Area

_225-

WESTERN AREA
Watford Police Station, Shady Lane, Watford, Herts, WD17 1DD
Tel: 01923 472000   Fax: 01923 472039

Creating a Safer Hertfordshire

5.   'Police letter that contradicts Grundy's claims.'

I decided to go and see George Galloway MP at his surgery office just off Brick Lane. He was my local elected Member of Parliament. I went twice to his surgery and on both occasions he wasn't even there. "On holidays in Portugal" I was told by one of his assistants and he promised he would tell George to write to the Chief Constable on my behalf and contact me with the results. I never heard a thing.

I wrote to the local Hemel Hempstead MP to see if he could help. I knew the police had to reply to an MP, the problem was finding one who would help me. Maybe an MP would get answers as to why the police were ignoring my letters, my solicitor's letters and all other forms of correspondence I tried to use. Tony McWalter MP took up my case and wrote to Hertfordshire Constabulary. I received a reply from Chief Superintendent Chris Taylor and to my horror the allegations had changed. The original allegation by PC Hughes of why I was removed from my home was because I was 'not on the deeds of the property'. That was changed to a second allegation by a Sergeant Huffer at Hemel police station to 'possible breach of the peace' and now a third allegation of why I was removed was because it was, 'a potentially violent situation'. But the superintendent's letter had a major contradiction in it. *'Police Officers do not have powers to formally evict anybody from premises and would need a relevant court order to do so'*. Why did the officers evict me without an order and why were their superiors continuing to defend the officers' actions? Nobody seemed to know. The Chief Superintendent's letter used language to insinuate that something could have happened but yet he made it sound as if it had already happened. The police excuses became more and more ridiculous. *'It was Mr Mahon's own decision to leave the house. The officers were only there to assist him'*. This was now the new claim police were stating.

My solicitor, Mr Roberts, continued with my claim against Liz while I pursued the police matter myself. Mr Roberts like so many others thought I was crazy to even try to take on the police. He said, "The police make the law up as they go along". But I didn't believe that. I thought he just couldn't be bothered to take the trouble to help me with my obsession to clear my name. I still hadn't realised at this point how determined the police could be to protect their good name.

New dates for my beneficial interest claim were set for the 10 and 11 of August 2005 at Watford County Court because Liz's lawyers wanted to adjourn from the original dates in May 2005. But the dates in August were also adjourned and rescheduled for November 2005. I didn't understand why there were so many delays. It seemed to me Liz was avoiding a court appearance.

I arrived at Mr Roberts's office in Old Street for a preliminary meeting before going on to discuss my case with the barrister who would be representing me in court. Mr Roberts was too busy so he sent his junior assistant instead. A tall gangly guy that resembled a bag of golf clubs; that's how he appeared to me and I could never remember his name. When he walked, everything rattled and when he stooped over everything fell out of his pockets.

We climbed into a black cab and he fell on his arse because he misjudged where the seat was inside the taxi. I was worried what he might do if he came to court with me. I sat in the cab thinking that travelling in a taxi was much more civilised than pedalling on my bike but of course I was too stupid to realise all this would be on my solicitor's bill. When he suggested we take a cab I thought he was going to pay. If I had have known I was paying I would have thrown him on the crossbar of my bike or insisted we take a bus. He had also informed me that Liz made an offer of £15,000 and so I felt confident that Liz was now getting worried. But that was two days ago and he was now saying he was thinking of asking Liz's solicitor to make an offer. The stupid bugger got things mixed up. There was no offer from Liz at all.

The meeting with the barrister lasted three hours. He was a little man with a massive office and a full head of dark hair. His name was James Parrington-Smith and he reeked of money. When I saw his fee then I knew why he smelt rich. He said I had a fifty/fifty chance of winning. He wasn't putting his reputation on the line with odds like that but I was to discover later that most barristers say fifty /fifty until they reach the court and then suddenly the odds change. "Take an out of court settlement. You're going to lose", was the advice I was to hear when we arrived at court. I told him I was only asking for the money I had put into my home and I was not interested in a share of the house. "Take as much as you can get," he laughed, "I just want to make sure you get your fair share." But according to Liz, I had eaten my fair share.

I was then asked to stand outside while Mr Parrington-Smith and the junior gangly solicitor had a quick private chat about my case. That made me very suspicious and confused. "Why?" I thought. "It's my case so why can't I listen to what's being said," and then the deadly demon of doubt crept into my mind about the barrister. But what could I do?

I was in the hands of the legal professionals and I expected them to do everything for my best outcome. But I still had doubts. They could screw it up and I would be left holding the bill. That's what happened to me back in the 1980's when my manager had a meeting with Riva Records, a company that was interested in signing me to their label. Whatever happened at that meeting, I never found out, but the Record Company decided not to sign me after talking to my manager. So I had good reason with my experiences not to trust others who represent me.

I decided to fly home to the more peaceful environment of Northern Ireland for a couple of days to visit my family and friends and to get away from the complexities of a legal system I didn't understand. I gave my cousin Clare a big hug and when she said, "welcome home," I felt that this was the place where I should be, away from my legal entanglement in England. I borrowed her car and drove around exploring. I stood on Gallows Hill overlooking the town of Downpatrick staring at a view that hadn't changed much in 30 years and remembering the summers I ran through the fields with my little black and brown mongrel dog called, Bullet, which was a stupid name to be shouting during the Troubles. As I stood there thinking over what had happened I felt I had reached a point in my life where I was fighting a system that didn't care who was telling the truth. One lie and everyone within the judicial authorities was jumping on the bandwagon to accuse me. How did it come to this?

I had brought Liz to Northern Ireland in 2002 when we were both so much in love and now I was standing alone on Strangford quayside watching the turbulent, fast flowing waters of the Lough swirling round like the memories in my head. I felt like the only person on the planet without the woman that had meant the world to me. The town appeared to be completely deserted on that drizzly April morning and that suited my mood. This was also the town where my first group played our first big gig at the Strangford Summer Carnival. I stood gazing at the hill where five 15-year-old kids ran down the slope to play in the big marquee. Tony Blaney, Michael Edgecombe, Andre Wilding, Gerry Kelly and me. Our band uniform was bell-bottom psychedelic trousers that had big yellow flowers and a turquoise blue jacket that had been stitched together out of curtain material by a little girl from the Green High, Caroline Cleland. She must have been a genius with a sewing machine to put a band uniform together that managed to make us all look so outrageous. We thought we were going to be bigger than the Beatles but then you do at 15.

I drove back into Downpatrick to visit an old friend of mine, Bobbie Hanvey. Bobbie has his own local radio show and was also a photographer who photographed many well-known faces in Northern Ireland. I banged on his front door that was on the busy main road into the town and when it opened I immediately noticed he still had his Afro ginger hair but not quite as thick as when he was younger.

"Jesus Christ, Pete Mahon, you scared the fuck out of me! I thought the door was being kicked in by the RUC," smiled Bobbie while grabbing my hand and giving it a firm shake. "Howya doin' you big long lanky string of shite?"

"Hello Bobbie."

"Come in, come in. It's good to see you."

Now I hadn't seen Bobbie for years and the first thing he said to me was, "Could you take this parcel to the post office for me? I can't be bothered to go myself." Of course I said "yes."

We talked about the good old days and then I told him about my split with Liz and my troubles with the police. I confessed to him the terrible time I was having and how it seemed to me that the whole world was against me. I told him how I was stressed, fed up and felt like crap. I started moaning that my home telephone had been cut off, my car had been broken into and the radio stolen. I was cycling everywhere on an old beaten-up pushbike that was given to me because I had no money. I didn't have a girlfriend either and had no desire to have one. I couldn't sleep, couldn't eat and couldn't think straight. He immediately stopped me and told me to give up. "If you're having sleepless nights then don't do it. Don't get involved with anything that's going to give you fuckin' sleepless nights because I wouldn't." And that was Bobbie's advice.

But I was determined to expose the corruption I felt was within Hertfordshire police. I had even decided I was going to find a private detective to help me find more evidence because I knew I would kick myself for the rest of my life if I didn't try something. Bobbie immediately told me not to get a private eye because he had a friend who hired a private investigator to spy on his wife and he ended up also sleeping with her.

"As they say in X Files, trust fuckin' no one," said Bobbie.

He told me to write to Sir Ronnie Flanagan, former chief Constable of the RUC, who was now Inspectorate of Constabulary that oversees all police forces in England.

"Tell him you're a friend of mine," insisted Bobbie.

But when I visited my good friend Tweedie he told me to ignore Bobbie's advice and write to Ian Paisley instead. Everyone had a solution to my problem. When I spoke to my old band mate Tony Blaney, who went off to join the RUC when I went to London to make records, he had another piece of advice, "Give up!" All this friendly advice was leading nowhere. Tony explained that the police supervisors would probably tell the two officers "not to do it again" and therefore nothing more would be done.

I did write to Sir Ronnie when I returned to England but as with so many letters I wrote seeking support and advice, his reply was meaningless.

Dear Mr Mahon, whilst our primary role is to scrutinise the performance of individual police forces, we are not routinely empowered to intervene in the police response to specific incidents. Should you wish to make a formal complaint about one or more of the officers involved in the incident you should write to the Chief Constable of Hertfordshire.

I felt like screaming, "I did that and my complaint was ignored. I am trying to complain about the whole of Hertfordshire Police and that's why I'm writing to you." No wonder I was having sleepless nights when

I'm receiving stupid advice from people who are suppose to know better. Maybe I should have written to Ian Paisley, but I didn't.

I went back to speak to my solicitor about my forthcoming claim against Liz and he started shouting at me.

"You've got to stop being so negative," he snapped. "If you turn up at court with that attitude you'll lose."

I just didn't know what to say. I was shocked. I'm paying this man a lot of money and he's yelling at me.

"What can I do?" I asked.

He hesitated. Maybe he realised I was in a state of mental numbness or maybe he was trying to rile me up to find out if I would retaliate and start shouting and swearing at him.

"Just tell the truth, that's all you can do," he calmly replied.

His only concern, I suppose, was to present a winning case; meanwhile his star witness was looking and acting like a man already with the rope around his neck waiting for the chair to be kicked away.

CHAPTER 10

◇◇◇◇◇

I'm Becoming Desperate

I came up with the bright idea, or so I thought at the time, to go to the Metropolitan police and ask them to investigate the two officers from Hertfordshire Constabulary and also Liz. It would be cheaper for me to get them to investigate rather than hiring a private detective. What had I to lose? If I could persuade them to give my complaint a crime number, then they would have to investigate.

My now legal advisor and confidante, Simon Groom, accompanied me to the Old Street Police Station. Simon was as keen as I was to find out what another police force would say if we requested their assistance. The reception area is a port-a-cabin and immediately I was reminded of the police stations in Belfast through the period known as the Troubles. It was a security precaution in Northern Ireland to prevent bombers reaching the main building. Blowing up a port-a-cabin is much cheaper for the government to replace than having to build a whole new police station. But in Northern Ireland there were lots of sandbags stacked around the building and barb wire everywhere. No sandbags here at Old Street just a bunch of young coppers who looked pricklier than any barb wire. I spoke to one young female uniformed officer and handed her a copy of my complaint. She studied it for a few minutes and then spoke to one of her male colleagues. They both appeared to be unsure what I was asking them to do.

"I'm afraid there is nothing we can do about this sir," she said

"Why?"

"It's outside our jurisdiction."

"I'm reporting a crime that has been committed by two Hertfordshire· police officers and I would like it to be investigated by an independent police force."

She insisted that she could not accept my complaint. I then insisted on seeing an honest officer who knows the law. Simon started laughing.

"I know the law, sir," she said

"In that case, maybe you can advise me if these officers committed misfeasance or malfeasance?"

She looked blank and then slightly embarrassed.

"I must warn you sir, not to start harassing me."

"What?" I said, "I have a witness here with me and he has seen that I am not harassing anyone. I only asked a question. Is this misfeasance or malfeasance?"

"I don't know sir. I'm just a PC. I'll see if I can find a detective who will see you".

Now I was getting somewhere.

We were kept waiting from 5.30pm to 8.30pm watching drug addicts, undesirables and people who didn't have a clue or an ounce of common sense stumble into the port-a-cabin to ask for police advice. They didn't even know why they were making complaints most of the time and just seemed to be looking for something to do. It kept us amused watching the many types that visit a police station. I was starting to think I had led a sheltered life.

Eventually we were taken into the main building, passing through the courtyard that was jam-packed with hundreds of stolen bicycles and up some stairs to a dingy office on the first floor. The detective, who was allocated to us, was young and cocky. He explained why he could not accept my request to investigate. He nonchalantly stretched back in his office chair and told us to go to Hertfordshire to report the crime because Metropolitan police only investigate Metropolitan police. When I told him I wanted an independent police force to investigate another police force he laughed and said, "We don't do independent investigations". This was a logical explanation to him but to me it was like George Bush proudly stating that he would investigate himself to prove his decision to go to war was 'just'. Simon and I argued with him for about an hour and then decided it wasn't worth continuing and left totally dissatisfied. Simon suggested I take the police to court, as he considered that to be the only way to get justice.

The next day I cycled off to the Royal Courts of Justice on the Strand to get some information on how to make an application to sue the police. I cycled through the city avoiding pedestrians and cars and wobbling between buses in Threadneedle Street. The street is so narrow that trying to ride a bike with a great big double-decker bus coming at you from the other direction and a white transit van up your arse, it could be compared to trying to thread an elephant through the eye of a needle.

Maybe that's why it's called Threadneedle Street. The street is famous for being the location of the Bank of England but the bank is no help to me. They say money talks - all my money seems to do is say nothing and wave goodbye since I've started employing solicitors.

As I continued cycling I heard a voice shout from behind. "Hey! You on the bike!"

I stopped and turned to see a big city copper coming towards me. Do I run or do I stand and face him?

"What do you think you're doing?" he asked.

"Riding my bike." I said, trying to play dumb.

"Yes, but what have you just done that was wrong?"

"Um? Didn't give a hand signal?"

"No, try again".

"Um? I suppose… it wasn't because I rode on the wrong side of that bollard, was it?"

"No supposing about it," he said sternly, "I could book you for that."

Should I argue and tell him I couldn't get past the bollard because the buses are too big for the street or the street is too narrow or even the bollard is in the wrong place or my bike has a mind of its own? No, I just couldn't be bothered to even try and explain why I did what he had witnessed.

He stood there looking at me in silence. I hung my head, staring at the ground waiting for his verdict. I had tried this with PC Hughes on the night of my eviction and it hadn't worked but I didn't know what else to do.

"I'll let you off this time but don't let me catch you doing it again."

And off he walked. I was surprised because I was convinced he was going to book me, arrest me or even accuse me of something serious. In the frame of mind, I was in I actually expected to be arrested. I thought he was going to accuse me of a serious motoring offence.

When I arrived at the Royal Courts I discovered there was a Citizens Advice Bureau just off the big main entrance hall. Just what I'd been looking for so I went to the door. A sign said it was open on Mondays, Wednesdays and Fridays but unfortunately today was Tuesday.

The next morning, I was there at 8am even though the bureau didn't open until 10am. I was going to make sure I was seen. There was a small collection of people already waiting outside at the gates and they appeared to be seasoned advice seekers. We all stood around on the pavement looking like a small group of agitators protesting against something. Nine o'clock and the gates to the court opened and there was a mad dash inside and a disorderly queue formed outside the Citizens Advice bureau door.

"I was here before you!" shouted one old lady.

"Like hell you were, lady," replied a Greek man. "I have been outside this building since half past seven this morning."

"No you haven't."

"Yes I have!"

Then the pushing and shoving started. As I stared at this amateur-wrestling match I was amazed at how desperate people can become to get some free advice. I turned to a Japanese woman who seemed as bewildered as I was at this pair of geriatrics in full battle and I shrugged my shoulders. She looked worried so I pulled out of my bag a packet of Japanese sweets that I had been given by a friend who had just come back from Japan. Her eyes lit up and she took one. I thought they tasted horrible and I was glad to get rid of them. To me they were like sucking seaweed mixed with a taste of sugar.

We started to discuss our reasons for being there. She needed advice about a neighbour from hell and I needed advice on the hell I was in. After we chatted for a while she invited me to one of her Buddhist meetings assuring me that chanting would help me with my struggle. Her name was Masako and she ended up becoming one of my most loyal supporters and I became a supporter of her struggle.

Meanwhile as we stood in the queue, the old lady was threatening to sue the Greek man for jumping in front of her and I thought to myself, "Well, we're all in the right place for suing."

Luck was on my side that day because some people got bored waiting and decided to leave. I was seen by one of the duty solicitors.

CHAPTER 11

◇◇◇◇◇

NOT A HOPE IN HELL

I climbed the big stone staircase following the young receptionist towards the second floor of this medieval looking building. On first glance she looked attractive but her attitude and blunt manner put a cold dampness on that attraction. Maybe she was fed up showing people up and down these grand stairs to the Citizens Advice solicitor who was stuck in a tiny office conversion that resembled a walk-in wardrobe. Her voice then broke my perturbing thoughts; "Wait here please" and she went in through a large wooden door.

The corridors of the Royal Courts of Justice are large and architecturally magnificent. I found the place intriguing but also frightening because I could hear the echoes of the law of the land reverberate around me. It's scary thinking what might happen if my case ended up here.
I looked out through the lead-lined window expecting to see a magnificent view of London but all I could see was a small flat roof covered in pigeon dirt.

I looked at my papers to make sure I had all the relevant information to hand when a woman, looking like she was suffering from a cold or even flu opened the large door.

"Mr Mahone?"

"It's pronounced…" and then I stopped myself. What's the point? I've been trying to educate the English for nearly 20 years on how to pronounce my name. If I tried for another 20 they still wouldn't get it right.

She introduced herself as 'Ann' one of the duty solicitors and then she blew her nose. "What can I do for you?" I had the choice of sitting on my chair in the opened doorway or placing my bum on the table if I wanted the door closed so I left the door open. I went into my spiel, as I had done so many times before, telling her about Liz and the two officers and how they had evicted me. She appeared to be trying to listen but I could tell that part of her brain was somewhere else.

"Sorry, I have a stinking cold today", she said and then started telling me that she was also in dispute with her ex-partner over their property. I tried to be sympathetic but that only encouraged her to continue into her disastrous life with men. Even though I tried to divert the conversation back to my matter she continued telling me how long she had studied law and how it had got her nowhere. When she told me that she was employing another solicitor to deal with her case I started to worry. She moaned about her failed marriage, her nutty lodger and her unstable boyfriend. I wasn't sure if this woman would last the duration of our meeting. When I made a joke that all the good men had been snapped up she agreed and said her mother had advised her to find a widower. She then gave me a long vacant stare. Why is she looking at me like that? I'm not a widower. I hoped she's not thinking what I think she might be thinking. I quickly started looking through my papers for my next question, then she looked at her watch and said, "I'm afraid your time's up."

"Hang on a minute!" I thought. "I haven't received any advice yet." I felt I'd just been used as an agony Aunt. So I quickly threw another question at her. "Which law have these two police officers broken?" She turned and picked up the phone. Then suddenly she sounded relieved when the receptionist told her that I was the last person she would be seeing that morning. She put the phone down and told me I could have another 10 minutes.

"You're being very generous," I thought to myself, "considering you've just spent 15 minutes telling me about your hell of life." She was making my problem sound like a camping holiday. She said the officers were probably in breach of Article 8 of the European Convention on Human Rights but before she advised me what I should do next she rubbed her forehead and told me to make another appointment.

"What about this afternoon?" I asked. She didn't laugh. She said she wanted a chance to look into it before she made a decision. I left her office not really sure what I had received; probably her flu, it certainly wasn't her advice.

The following week I returned only to be allocated a different duty solicitor, Virginia Fu, a Chinese/English woman who appeared more on the ball than Ann. Her friendly and articulate explanations gave me comfort for the first time in months. I was starting to feel relaxed in her company. She advised me to apply for a bar *pro bono* barrister to represent me. I didn't know what a *pro bono* barrister was. She explained that *pro bono* barristers give a certain amount of their time for nothing and help with advice and representation in court. But she warned me that taking on the police can be a daunting and sometimes impossible task. I decided to ignore the word 'impossible'. At last I had found someone who seemed to want to help me. We sat and filled out the form to apply for a barrister together and then Virginia told me she would post it but

I immediately said, "Why post it when I can take it there myself. I have my bike." She told me to make another appointment with the receptionist and she would see me next week. Off I skipped down the stairs.

The receptionist informed me that I could only make an appointment by phone. I stood there for a second then I turned and walked out the door, took out my mobile and punched in the number. I could hear the phone ringing on the other side of the door. It rang and rang. "Why is she not picking up? I know she's there." Then a voice eventually answered, "RCJ advice bureau."

"Hello. I would like to make an appointment for next week, please."

"Certainly, what's your name?"

"Peter Mahon and I'm the man standing outside your door."

"Okay Mr Mahon, let me see. I can offer you next Wednesday at 10.30am."

"I'll take it."

As I walked towards the main door to the street a woman approached me and asked if I was having legal problems. "Yes," I said. She then offered me a glass stone the size of a 50 pence coin. "Take this and keep it somewhere warm and it will bring you luck." She placed it in my hand and stood smiling. "Don't leave it in the dark. Keep it somewhere bright and warm." I thanked her and continued walking out the door

Date: 4th January 2006
Your Ref:
Our Ref: PSD/C0/00404/05
Contact: Indira Patel
Tel: 01707 638452

Mr Peter Mahon
████████████
████████████
████████████

Dear Mr Mahon

Complaint Against Police

Further to our telephone conversation on the 3rd January 06, I am writing to confirm that PC Hughes resigned on the 22nd December 2005. In light of this information, although we can invite PC Hughes to be interviewed, we cannot compel him as he is no longer an employee and subject to the Police Code of Conduct.

We can still investigate the issues you raised against the other two officers subject to the complaint. However as there is no criminal allegation against PC Hughes, they can be no sanction imposed against him.

I hope this makes matters clear.

Yours sincerely,

Mrs Indira Patel BSc (Hon's) DMS
Investigator
Professional Standards Department

Police Headquarters, Professional Standards Dept, Stanborough Road, Welwyn Garden City, Herts AL8 6XF
Tel: 01707 354548 Fax: 01707 354549

6.   'Letter from Professional Standards informing me of PC Hughes resignation to avoid investigation.'

into the street. I looked at the stone in the sunlight and it sparkled like a diamond. I wasn't sure why she had given the stone to me but I took it home and placed it on top of my television by the window so it was getting sunlight and heat. I was taking no chances because I needed all the luck I could get.

It was now November 2005. I received a letter from the Independent Police Complaints Commission (IPCC) stating they had instructed the police to investigate my complaint into the action of the two officers, PC Hughes and PC Thurston. A few weeks later the police then contacted me and said that Professional Standards would commence the investigation in December. I was over the moon because I thought now the truth would come to light. But then one of the officer's, PC Gordon Hughes suddenly handed in his resignation. I was told Professional Standards would not interview him even though they had four weeks to place a Regulation 9 order on him before he actually left the police force. The order would have enabled Professional Standards to force Hughes to be questioned. They said, "There was no point."

"No point!" I shouted. They didn't seem to realise that the point is to find out why he evicted me.

The investigation of PC Hughes and PC Thurston turned into a farce. Professional Standards didn't want to interview any of my witnesses and didn't even want to interview me but I insisted. They took statements from Liz and PC Thurston. They even took a statement from Palfrey. Why they took a statement from him was beyond me. He wasn't even there when I was evicted. The whole thing was looking very suspicious, not only to me but to everyone else. Professional Standards also refused to take a statement from John Hooper, the next door neighbour who had witnessed the police officers arrive and leave.

A meeting, which I had insisted on, to interview me, was eventually arranged in Hitchin Police station with two Professional Standards investigating officers. It was a cold December morning as I drove to Luton to pick up Simon and then continue our journey onto Hitchin. I was feeling confident and looking forward to hearing what Professional Standards had to say for themselves.

I was sure now that the two officers would be prosecuted. We met with a Ms Patel and a Mr How. Ms Patel said very little but Mr How had lots to say. He told us that nothing can be done or will be done to the two officers and he wasn't interested whether Liz had lied or not. I thought it was a crime to lie to the police and to waste police time but he insisted that it was not. He sat back in his chair, played with a rubber band and smiled like a delinquent schoolboy. Ms Patel looked like she was completely lost during the whole interview but Mr How arrogantly told her what to write and where to write it on the form. It was a bizarre meeting, more like a training session for Ms Patel. I could see that Professional Standards were not taking this complaint seriously enough. As we left, Simon said the whole meeting was a joke and he felt it was a complete waste of time but I felt I had put a very strong case forward and I was optimistic that I would achieve something from the meeting.

It was March 2006 before Professional Standards completed their investigation and concluded my complaint was unsubstantiated. As far as they were concerned no one had done anything wrong. I wrote an appeal to the IPCC but they agreed with the Professional Standards findings. I slowly became aware that I only had two choices: Appeal in the High Courts for a Judicial Review against the IPCC's decision or give up. I decided to apply to the High Court.

Meanwhile, the day of reckoning between Liz and me had arrived. One year on and we were to appear for the second time at Watford County Court to decide if I will receive any money from Liz. It all seemed so pointless now. What I wanted a year ago was not really what I wanted now. I was hoping Liz would back down and admit she had lied to the police. I didn't care if I got money or not I just wanted my name cleared. I collected my daughter Jenna from her home in Holloway Road and we drove to Watford that is about 10 miles north of London. I was starting to hate the drive there because of the hours I had spent going back and forth researching through court papers and investigating statements to find some clues to why the police were dragging this matter on. It seemed I was having so many disappointments every time I went there but Watford had a great cafe opposite the court buildings and I loved the grilled chicken with the mashed potatoes they served. That was something to look forward to.

We were the first ones in the court house and so we sat in the waiting room. I felt tense and Jenna sat yawning. Liz arrived and this time she had an entourage from her work with Laura her daughter and a solicitor. Palfrey wasn't with her. My solicitor's assistant, the tall gangly one, arrived and took us into a side room to discuss our case. He was half way through his advice when my barrister, Mr Parrington-Smith walked in and apologised for his late arrival. He then immediately advised me to go for a settlement out of court.

"Why?" I asked

"You have a very small chance of winning. If you want to walk away from court with some money in your pocket, you should try to settle."

I sat there, not quite sure why he was telling me to settle out of court when six months earlier he had told me I had a good chance of winning. I got up and looked out the window. I struggled with my decision: should I go into court or should I settle? If only there was someone in the room that could tell me the best thing to do. Jenna told me to settle. She was frightened I would lose.

"But what about all the evidence I've got?"

"What evidence?" the barrister asked.

Had he mixed up my case with someone else's or had he even bothered to look at the paper work? All the receipts of materials I had bought, all the bills I had paid, the telephone and the repairs I had done and the letter that Liz had written on my behalf, without my knowledge, to remove my name from the mortgage agreement. "She'll say you instructed her to write it." And that was that. The work I'd done investigating and the days I sat on the computer writing statements now appeared to have been a total waste of time. I didn't know what to say. I felt I was fighting with this barrister who I'm paying to fight for me.

"What would you settle for?" he asked

"I don't want a share of the house, just the £20,000 I put into the property. But if she is prepared to admit she lied to the police then I don't want any money."

"I can ask but I can't see you getting that," he said. "Try for £10,000."

"No, I want £20,000 or an admission she lied."

"Okay, I'll go and see what they say".

Ten minutes later he came back with an offer.

That night I went to the Royal Oak pub in Columbia Road where my friend Steve Latner had organised a get-together with the gang from the photographer's club to celebrate my anticipated victory.

"Well, did you win?" asked Guy

"I did and I didn't."

"And?"

"We didn't go into court. We negotiated for about half an hour, she settled and I got some money."

"That's alright then."

"The barrister said I was the winner but I don't feel like a winner."

"You got your money," said Steve.

"Well not really, I only got £7,000."

"That's all right," said Guy.

"Yeah, the barrister said he didn't want her to screw any more money out of me and she's the one who has to sign a cheque. But I had to pay him and the solicitor so I feel like I've spent a pound to earn a penny. Liz was an expensive woman to sleep with."

"I went out with a girl once who told me I was the first man she had ever slept with," interrupted Steve, "I was quite chuffed until she said all the others had stayed awake."

Everyone laughed except me. I was numb. That feeling in your mouth when you've been to the dentist and had a tooth extracted. You know it's for the best but you still have a tooth missing.

As everyone drank and chatted I couldn't help thinking was it all worth it. Liz and I could have come to a similar agreement over a cup of tea and neither of us would have had the trauma and financial stress of going to court. It wasn't really about money, it was more about justice and that feeling you get when you've achieved success. I needed to finish this. I wanted to sue the police for making false allegations about me but I knew it was going to be a much harder task. I wanted to prove that the IPCC had got it wrong because the police had got it wrong and therefore that would prove Liz had lied. But I was wrong. Everyone thought I should be suing Liz instead of the police but I considered the police to be the incompetent ones who continued blindly to make false allegations. Confirmation bias it's called. That's the official term and it means the tendency to search for and interpret information in a way that confirms one's pre-existing beliefs or hypotheses. The police wanted to prove they were right and were prepared to do anything, even lie to prove they were right. I knew they were trying to wear me down. As long as the police continued to defend Liz I had no chance of persuading a judge that Liz was lying.

"I don't think you have much of a hope in suing the police," said Guy.

"You're not the only one who's told me 'not a hope in hell'," I said, and then I went off to spend the rest of the evening drinking like a dehydrated elephant.

CHAPTER 12

◇◇◇◇◇

When It Rains It Pours

The year 2007 was, I suppose, eventful. I had two offers of marriage and two High Court appearances.

In 40 years I have never had a proposal of marriage but in one year, within a matter of months, I had two. As the saying goes, women are like buses, they all come at once. I once had a young woman ask me out on the top deck of a double decker bus when I first arrived in London and another who wanted to sleep with me because she was drunk and thought the end of the world was coming and of course Liz. Look how that turned out but I was never offered marriage, even from Liz.

The first offer was from a happy-go-lucky West Indian woman. We were working together in an old people's Day Care Centre near where I lived. I had taken the part-time job to help earn some money to keep my head above water. I was using most of my time researching, investigating and writing statements and not bothering to earn money. I had given up being concerned about making a proper living because I wanted to concentrate fighting my battle with the legal system. I was still doing some solo gigs to earn a little bit of money but my heart wasn't really into it anymore. I was sick to death having drunken Irishmen requesting Irish songs I'd never heard of and songs I couldn't even be bothered to learn. I missed the camaraderie of playing in a group.

The hazards of singing in some London Irish pubs is having the nerve to stand in front of a bunch of drunks who all consider themselves to be Simon Cowell from X Factor. If an Englishman didn't like me he would generally get up and walk out but if a drunken Irishman didn't like me he would stay all night and tell me how bad I was. The Irishmen I've encountered don't tell me where to go; first they'll ask me where I'm from and then tell me where to go. It can be a long confusing night.

The majority of the old people in the Day Care Centre where I was working were women in their 70's, 80's and 90's and a lively bunch they were too.

"Young man," I would hear one old dear shout.

"Yes Margaret," I would reply, "and what can I do for you?"

"Would you like to come back to my place for a nice cup of tea?"

"Ooh and what else?" I joked.

"What ever you want!" she replied.

"You dirty woman!" I replied. "I'll be 'round tonight."

And then they would all burst out laughing before going into fits of coughing, asthma attacks and convulsions. The staff would then panic to put them in the recovery position. Maybe they did it on purpose to receive the 'kiss of life.'

The West Indian woman was due to lose her job because her work permit was about to expire. She was willing to pay me just to marry her and the offer was very tempting as I needed the money to help finance my case but I was also hoping to claim Legal Aid and to get married to her would affect my claim. I would be assessed with our joint incomes. The second proposal was from an attractive Chinese student, a girl in her mid 20's whom I had rented my spare room to. This proposal could have also been tempting but there was no money offered.

"Do you realise what would happen if we were found out?" I told her. "You would be deported and I could go to jail."

"I can't afford to pay you," she said.

And I couldn't afford to take the chance. So I married neither of them.

My first High Court appearance in March was like a fumbling one-night stand, brief and unsatisfying. I was so dismayed at the IPCC agreeing with the Professional Standards investigation that the two police officers had done nothing wrong, I wanted to appeal against the IPCC's decision. I applied to the Royal Courts of Justice hoping to be granted a Judicial Review against the IPCC. I had no representation, didn't have a clue what procedures were required and was just hoping the judge would see how the IPCC had got things wrong. That was my first big mistake. When I stood up to speak to the judge, my mind told me to stop but yet my mouth continued to talk at a speed faster than sound. I wasn't sure what I was trying to say but yet I continued talking hoping I would talk my way into something coherent. Maurice and Simon sat beside me whispering and passing notes while I tried unsuccessfully to ignore the distractions and answer all the points that Mr Buckett, the barrister representing the IPCC, was giving. As well as being confused, I was trying to read the bits of paper being flung at me. Behind me were

Caolan, Jenna, Masako and the Chinese girl, waiting for the performance of a lifetime. I had a lot of supporters but unfortunately no skill to impress them. I felt like the singer who couldn't sing. I had prepared myself for a hearing about being granted an extension of time because as far as the IPCC were concerned I had not made my court application by the correct date. Mr Buckett was trying to persuade the judge to abandon the case while I was desperately trying to explain why my documents had been submitted late.

"I was given the wrong date by the clerk in the Applications office," I pleaded, "and I have a letter from him to prove that."

The judge, to my surprise, accepted my explanation and just as I sat down with a sigh of relief, Mr Buckett went into his speech accusing me of shouting and swearing at the officers.

"Wait a minute!" I heard a voice in my head say, "what's this got to do with my application being submitted late?"

As Mr Buckett listed point after point, accusation after accusation I froze for a moment and then realised I should be writing these points down. Maurice and Simon were frantically shuffling bits of paper to and fro. "Stop!" I heard the voice in my head shout. "Stop and ask the judge what this hearing is about."

"This is not what you were prepared for," I heard Maurice whisper.

But I couldn't stop my mouth from replying to Mr Buckett's accusations.

I fumbled through my notes that now meant nothing, I stuttered out sentences that sounded gibberish and I stood there in my grey suit looking like the best man at a wedding who didn't even know who the bride and groom were.

"I will deliver my verdict after lunch," the judge concluded, "court resumes at 2.15."

"All rise," shouted the clerk of the court.

I stood there feeling like a plucked chicken waiting to be stuffed and put in the oven as my supporters gathered round to sprinkle their sympathy on me.

"Well, I made a right cock up of that," I mumbled.

"You were fine, Dad," said Jenna.

"This is not what you were told the hearing was about," repeated Maurice. "It was meant to be a hearing to grant permission for an extension of time."

But whether we had all read the order wrongly or misunderstood the letter from the court, the hearing was now over.

We lunched in the court cafe among all the barristers in their gowns and the solicitors with their clients.

"I wish I had a barrister," I sighed.

"Too late for that now," shouted Simon, "I can't believe how fucking useless that IPCC barrister was, he couldn't string two fucking sentences together."

"But I was worse."

"It's not over yet," said Maurice, "Let's wait and see what the judge has decided."

We shuffled back into the court and waited for the judge's summing up. He did appear to be sympathetic to everything I had said and Jenna thought he looked kind. He started speaking and went on and on for 20 minutes about the grounds of criticism, alleged failures of the investigation, the lack of accounts from witnesses and the result of important evidence being left out. I just couldn't tell from the tone of his voice whether he was going to find in my favour or not. Then he finished with that dreaded word I was half expecting, "However..."
When a judge says that, you know its curtains.

"...for reasons which I have given, I consider that there is no reasonably arguable case for a judicial review here, and accordingly permission is refused."

"My Lord, before you rise, just one matter," interrupted Mr Buckett. "I am not instructed to apply for costs from the IPCC, however, in relation to the police; I am instructed to apply for £1400 worth of costs."

Why are the police looking for costs I thought? The greedy bastards! There had been some confusion when I had gone to the CAB (Citizens Advice Bureau) for advice whether the police should be named on the court application form or not but in the end I was advised to write IPCC and 'other'. Who the 'other' is was anyone's guess but the IPCC barrister obviously thought it was the police and so he tried to get costs for them. I sank into my seat expecting the judge to grant the police costs.

"I am not going to make an order for costs," replied the judge, "I do not consider it would be reasonable to make an order against Mr Mahon by Hertfordshire Constabulary."

I was shocked and immediately jumped up to ask for confirmation.

"Sorry, I just wondered what my situation is. Have I to pay costs or haven't I?"

"No, you do not have to pay costs."

"Do I have the option to appeal?"

"You can make an application to the court of appeal," said the Judge.

"Thank you very much, my Lord."

"That is a statement of fact, I am not giving permission."

I gave half a smile. I wasn't sure if it was appropriate to smile at a Judge or not.

"No costs and I can appeal so it's not over yet." I said out loud.

I immediately made my application to appeal and with the help of the CAB I continued to pursue the Bar *pro bono* Unit to get representation. This time I was going to try to bring legal help.

The next day I took a bus to the Royal Courts of Justice to apply for a fee exception. This would allow me to obtain a transcript copy of the judge's summing up for free. I needed his exact words to make my appeal and I couldn't really afford to pay the fee.

I arrived outside the courts at the same time as Paul McCartney who was also having partner problems in 2007. He was one of my childhood heroes when I listened to the Beatles records but I never expected to see him in person. He looked over and gave me a wave or maybe it was to the crowd of photographers I was standing beside. I went in to the fee exception office but Paul wasn't there. There were a lot of people and most of them looked wealthy enough to pay their legal costs while I on the other hand had just enough money to pay for a coffee in the cafe.

I waited in the queue for ages, at what I thought was the fee exception office and then was told I was at the wrong place. The man behind the counter told me to go to the Queens Building room WG08 to ask for the judge's approval. Apparently the judge has to approve the release of the court transcript. But when I got there another man told me to go to the Administrative office. I went back to the other end of the building and arrived at the Administrative office only to be told I had to go to the Appeals office and the people in the Appeals office sent me in search of Room E04. When I found Room E04 it turned out to be the fee exception office, the first place I had queued when I arrived. The man who had told me three hours earlier I was at the wrong office casually apologised and took my application. I had wasted nearly a whole day walking round that massive building looking for somewhere I had already been. I bet Paul McCartney didn't have any problems like that. The man behind the counter then told me he needed a recent bank statement from me.

"This is a recent bank statement," I said.

"It's a week old. I need a more recent one," he insisted.

So I fought my way out past the photographers at the front door and ran down the street looking for a Lloyds bank. I found one and came tearing back, out of breath, with a new mini statement I obtained from the Cash Machine (ATM). He accepted that mini statement and then stamped 'approved' on my application for fee exception. I would now be able to get a copy of the court transcript without paying the fee. I pushed my way out past the photographers at the front door again who were still waiting for Paul McCartney. I caught a bus home feeling exhausted.

Meanwhile, I still couldn't find a solicitor willing to help me apply for legal aid. One of the managers at the old people's centre advised me to contact the Newham Monitoring Project which help people with 'action against the police.' I went there and spoke to a woman whose name I couldn't pronounce and explained my dilemma in finding legal help but she said they usually only deal with immigrants, Blacks and Asian people who have experienced police harassment. I told her I was an Irish immigrant who had experienced police harassment and that made her hesitated for a moment.

"Well…" She didn't know what to say. "I suppose that would be okay." She phoned a couple of solicitors while I was there and left messages on their answer machines.

Later that day, a solicitor from the Newham Monitoring Project phoned me, saying he specialised in suing the police. He gave a short breakdown of his understanding of my case and then told me I would not get public funding because of the amount of money I would receive if I won. He estimated that my case would only pay out £3000 and to get legal aid I would need to be awarded more than £7000 if I won. He said I would be better off suing Liz, my ex-partner, but I would not be able to claim legal funding for an individual, only a public authority.

"It was Liz who caused this incident to happen and the police were only acting on her complaint," he said.

I felt devastated by those words and wanted to go to the first pub I could find and get blind drunk. I knew I couldn't sue Liz while she had the police backing up her story.

I had to prove the police lied to prove Liz lied and I still had the obstacle of the IPCC agreeing with the police. I was climbing a hill that was getting steeper and steeper. I started to realise why it was so difficult to sue the police.

A few weeks later the Citizens Advice Bureau (CAB) solicitor, Virginia Fu, informed me that I might have a *pro bono* barrister willing to represent me in my Judicial Review appeal against the IPCC. When I met the barrister, Mr Harvey (at his request I have agreed to use a pseudonym), my first impression was - he's too young, what does he know? But when we started discussing the evidence I had gathered, I was immediately impressed by his knowledge of my case. I had paid top barristers who knew less. It seemed he had read every letter and statement in my 200-page bundle. We talked for over three hours and even though his wife rang him twice, he continued with our meeting until he understood all the facts. He admitted he was still unsure if I had a strong enough case or not. But thankfully, he decided to take up the matter and was willing to represent me in court.

When I first started searching for a solicitor in London I was totally unaware of how difficult it was to get legal aid. I thought you just applied and that was it. But it was not that easy then and it's even more difficult now. I had literally come to the last solicitor on my list that specialized in suing the police and his office was in East Ham, not far from where I lived. When I phoned him he invited me into his office for a discussion. None of the other solicitors had invited me for any meetings but I didn't want to count my chickens before they had hatched. I turned up at his office in my best suit and my 50 pence briefcase I had found in a junk shop. Mr King was a young man, clean cut with spectacles but his office was a complete shamble. There were bundles of papers on his desk, on the shelves, on his cabinets, on the floor and even on the chair I was to sit on. He listened to my story and then asked me where I was from.

"Belfast," I said.

"I'm getting married to a girl from Belfast next year," he smiled.

We talked about Belfast for about 10 minutes and then he suddenly said, "I'll take your case on." He even agreed to apply for legal aid. Suddenly a day that seemed dull turned into a bright sunny experience. I skipped out of his office and ran all the way back to my car. I did wonder if he thought I had a good case or whether he was just helping me because he was marrying a girl from Belfast.

It was now September and as I stood, a lone figure, in the great hall at the Royal Courts of Justice I felt excited and nervous at the prospect of returning to court to try and get a judicial review against the IPCC. I had come a long way, further than a lot of people predicted. This was my second chance and this time I had legal representation. I had arrived early to be sure I didn't keep the barrister, Mr Harvey, waiting but he was late – very late; in fact I didn't think he was coming. Then he came charging towards me.

"Bugger!" he said as he approached, "I've forgotten my wig. I wonder if I can borrow one here."

"You need a wig?" I thought to myself, "We need to discuss my case, not worry about your bloody wig."

"I'll have to run back to the chambers and get it," he said, "I'm sorry, but I won't be long."

And off he ran. I stood there, feeling like a pea lost in a pile of potatoes, with barristers in wigs and gowns, solicitors in suits and piles of papers while dodgy looking people in track suits and jeans stared at me. "Please get him to the court on time!" I prayed. Then Simon, Masako and Jenna arrived.

"Is your barrister here yet?" asked Simon.

"No, he's gone home to get his wig."

"What!" shouted Simon, "what's the stupid fucker doing?"

"Don't worry Peter," said Masako, "I have a good feeling everything will be okay. I have been chanting for your success."

"Thank you." I said but thinking it may be a waste of time if I haven't got a barrister. "How long did you chant?"

"Seven days."

"My God, you must be exhausted?"

"It's important that you win and chanting will work."

"I hope so, if just for your sake."

"I've been praying too, Dad," smiled Jenna.

"Thank you, Jenna."

I felt so lucky that so many people were wishing me well and praying for my success. My cousin Clare was praying to some saint but I didn't catch his name. I thought she said saint Francis of Assisi but he's the patron saint of animals and I was wondering why she would be praying to him. Another friend was sending out spiritual healing vibrations to help me cope with the stress. Surely I was bound to win with all these good well-wishers. Masako looked so serious and appeared to be more concerned than I was about the hearing. My barrister returned with his wig and we all went into the courtroom. I was feeling so battered and bruised from all the disappointments over the last couple of years that my senses were expecting the worst. Mr Harvey stood up and began to introduce himself and explain the unfortunate reason why my case had come this far. The judge, Lord Justice Auld, interrupted and stopped him and said he didn't want to waste his time.

"I have decided to grant permission," he said.

Simon looked ecstatic, Mr Harvey looked surprised and I felt confused.

"I have read the papers with care," continued the judge, "including your skeleton argument on behalf of the applicant, Mr Mahon and having considered all of the evidence, I feel a great unease about the circumstances of this case. Given the information available beforehand to the officers, their conduct in awakening and removing Mr Mahon from his home in the middle of the night deserves a more vigorous and thorough investigation by Hertfordshire Constabulary. I grant the application."

Simon grabbed my hand and started shaking it vigorously. Everyone was smiling.

"What the...?" I gasped.

"You've won!" shouted Simon.

"Have I?"

I just didn't believe it.

"But...but...we have hardly begun."

"The judge has granted you a Judicial Review," Simon said.

"Wow!"

We came out of the courtroom and everyone was smiling and congratulating me. Mr Harvey looked excited too. He even admitted we had been on a 50/50 chance of winning. As we all headed for the court's cafe, Mr Harvey was talking 19 to the dozen and I couldn't keep up with what was being said. He was walking at a trotting pace while I was trying to keep up and listen at the same time. Simon and Jenna were following closely while poor Masako, in her shoes that were too tight, trailed along last.

"Can you slow down," I shouted, "I'm finding it hard to digest what you're saying."

Mr Harvey continued moving at a jogging pace down corridors that led to locked doors and then back upstairs that led back to where we had started. We passed Masako twice. As he talked and searched for the way out, we all blindly followed him, trying to find a route out of this maze of hallways, corridors and stairways and all the time he kept telling me what this victory could mean.

"We can now get legal aid with this judgement and a good solicitor, someone to recommend a QC," said Mr Harvey excitedly.

I had never seen him so energized.

"This is a precedent," Simon shouted, "no one has ever got a Judicial Review against the IPCC before."

We all eventually piled into the cafe and I ordered teas and coffees for everyone. I even splashed out and bought a sausage roll for Simon and Mr Harvey. I got a banana for myself to replace the lost energy from running round the building trying to keep up with the young barrister. With all the enthusiasm I didn't even notice that the girl behind the counter didn't give me the banana even though I had paid for it. I was on the bus home before I realised it.

As it turned out we didn't need to go back to court. The granting of a Judicial Review changed everything and the police were now forced to admit that the two officers had evicted me unlawfully.

Because the IPCC weren't prepared to continue the fight in court they offered a meeting with me in their head office at Holborn instead. Maurice offered to come with me.

My first impression of this controversial organisation was that their offices were enormous, with rows of people sitting at computers. After a drawn out security check, Maurice and I were taken into a small room to meet Neil Jasper and Jason Taylor. I brought my tape recorder just in case something was said that would be later denied. They admitted that this meeting with me was unusual and had never happened before. They conceded that mistakes had been made and were prepared to apologise but they refused to offer any money as compensation. I was promised that a full and detailed report would be sent to me within a couple of weeks. But no report was ever sent. Instead I received a one-page letter from Mike Franklin (IPCC Commissioner) saying that the police would look into my complaint. Mr Franklin said that PC Thurston would receive words of 'Manage Action' and that it would be explained to him 'how his actions did not meet the required standards.' But of course Thurston continued to say he had done nothing wrong. What a waste of words that was. Mr Franklin also told me that he would write to the Deputy Chief Constable suggesting a meeting with me. It took me a further 5 years pursuing the Deputy Chief Constable to have this meeting with him.

When I went home I worked out my costs, transport, phone calls, letters and time spent researching. I sent the IPCC a bill for £3000 but they said they would never pay that amount of money. Through the Citizens Advice Bureau (CAB) I was given the name of a Costs Lawyer, who specialises in working out costs for claimants. She worked out my bill to be £6000. We sent the bill to the IPCC and they offered me £3000, the amount I originally asked for and so I took the money.

My victory had changed everything and everyone was now taking my complaint more seriously. I bumped into my first solicitor, Mr Roberts in a café on Old Street a few weeks later and casually told him of my victory in the High Court. He nearly choked on his sandwich and stared at me with a look of disbelief.

As the year 2007 came to a close, I was feeling more confident and my achievement in the High Court helped me realise the work, time and money I had spent over the three previous years had been worth it.

CHAPTER 13

PRIVATE INVESTIGATIONS

Francis and Errol are two mechanics working from a back street garage off Hackney Road. They have repaired every car I've had since 1996; even when I moved to Hemel I still brought my car and Liz's car for servicing and repairs.

Francis, who calls himself a plastic Paddy because both his parents were Irish and he was born in England, has his head stuck inside every engine that comes into the garage. He says he was born on an American plane flying from Ireland to England so he's not sure what nationality he is meant to be.

Errol is a big black guy who charms every woman who passes his garage. He has had a varied career as a doorman, a debt collector, a private investigator and a mechanic and he was also chosen to be a torch bearer for the 2012 Olympics. Whenever I was visiting the garage Errol would give me his wisdom and knowledge on how to do some private detective work while Francis was fixing my car. Errol warned me that using a private detective to find where ex-PC Hughes lived would cost a lot of money and so he advised me to do the investigating myself. "Easier said than done," I said. But by ignoring Errol's advice I was led down dead end streets and fruitless searches for help. I needed to speak to Hughes to confirm he was the one who wrote the crime report that claimed I was abusive on the night I was evicted from my home.

When I started trawling the internet to find someone who would help me find Hughes, I soon realised that Errol was right; all private detectives were (a) not cheap and (b) not interested when I said I was looking for an ex-copper. Looking for an unfaithful ex-wife, they all wanted that job but an ex-copper, not interested. Some refused point blank, others said they were too busy and one slammed the phone down on me.

A conversation with the Hemel Hempstead MP, Mike Penning, revealed that Sergeant Huffer was now stationed at Berkhamsted Police station. He was the sergeant who refused to take my complaint when I went to Hemel Police station with my son Caolan, the day after I was evicted. I decided I should try to have a chat with him to see if I could gain some information or maybe discover where Hughes lived. My first visit was unsuccessful because he was on leave for four days. My second visit was ill-timed as he had just finished his shift and gone home. But my third visit was successful. I picked up the entry phone that was situated in the rear car park of the building because the police front reception was closed. It was the same in most smaller police stations, which were closed due to financial cuts. When I asked for Sergeant Huffer, a voice questioned me who was enquiring. I said I was advised to speak to him by Mike Penning MP and that was the key to let me in. I don't think he recognised me and he didn't show any signs of familiarity with my story. He took me through to the main office of the building and listened to my request for an explanation of why I had been evicted. We sat at the computer and he looked through the crime reports and showed me the logs but it didn't reveal anything I hadn't already known. I decided not to tell him what I really wanted to know and didn't mention anything about the way he had behaved on that day back in 2004. I resisted the temptation to accuse him of protecting a bent copper because I knew he wasn't going to assist me in any way with my investigations. So I decided to try to find someone else.

Eventually I found Reilly, (at his request I have agreed to use a pseudonym) a disillusioned actor who did a bit of detective work on the side and he was cheap. He found the ex-copper's address and even obtained his mobile telephone number. At last I was getting somewhere.

I sat in my car outside Hughes's address in Luton for hours and days and then weeks and most of the time I was bursting for a pee. I wonder if private detectives have urinary problems. I decided the only way to get to the truth was to confront ex-PC Hughes face to face. I followed a woman who I thought had come out of the side door of Hughes's house but she turned out to be the next door neighbour. It was a long time before I realised he didn't live at that address anymore. So I went back to Reilly who phoned Hughes's mobile number and pretended he was on the hunt for ex-police officers to do a top secret job in security. Hughes was suspicious at first but when Reilly gained his confidence with his acting skills, Hughes willingly parted with his address to send details of the 'none existing' job. He had fallen for the scam hook, line and sinker.

I went to the new address, a suburban area which was on the north-side of Luton with my new sidekick, Masako, who was excited at the thought of doing detective work. We parked at the end of his street around 7am and waited. Hughes appeared from the house with a woman, got into his car and drove off. I thought it was Hughes but I wasn't sure. He appeared to be a much skinnier man than I remembered with short hair and glasses. He didn't look anything like the police officer Hughes who had thrown me out of my home but then it had been four years since I'd last seen him so he may have changed. We followed closely behind and then he stopped at a bus stop to let the woman out of his car. He continued in the direction of Dunstable with us still in pursuit and drove into a B & Q builder's car park. We parked up and watched him go inside.

"What shall we do?" asked Masako.

"He might recognise me so perhaps you should follow him."

"What shall I do?"

"See what he does." I said, "He might work there or maybe he's just going to buy something, I don't know."

Masako went inside the store while I waited in the car. It seemed forever but after 30 minutes or so Hughes returned with a trolley load of wood. He loaded up and drove off. Masako was nowhere to be seen. Should I follow the ex-copper or go and look for Masako? But just then she appeared.

"I've lost him," she said. She hadn't brought her glasses with her and without them she was blind as a bat.

We went back to his house but his car wasn't there so I deduced from that he was working as a builder. I returned a week later, this time on my own, and parked my car outside a neighbour's house with a good view of Hughes's front door. I sat there all day waiting but no one appeared. A woman walked passed my car a couple times so I smiled and said "hello"; I thought it was best to be friendly. At around five o'clock the woman's husband arrived home and they stood talking and pointing towards me. He then approached me. He told me his wife had noticed I had been sitting outside their house all day and he wanted to know why. I had to think quickly – something I'm not that good at.

I jumped out of the car and told him I was watching someone in the street concerning benefit fraud. "I can't tell you which house obviously because I'm on a secret stake-out." He immediately asked for identification. I started searching through my pockets desperately trying to think of something that would look official to convince him that I was genuine. I pulled out my driving licence but luckily before I flashed my pretend ID, he started walking away and got into his car. I was now worried that he might phone the police to report a suspicious character hanging about so I moved my car to the bottom of the street and parked behind a van hoping I couldn't be seen. Half an hour later a car went past and drove into the driveway of number 28.

It was now 2008 and ex-PC Hughes had admitted when he had spoken with Reilly that he hadn't worked with the police for quite some time. His last action on duty was when the Bunsfield explosion in Hemel Hempstead happened in December 2005. My friend Johnny Baker phoned me from Huddersfield to tell me he saw the big fire on the news and remembered that's where I lived.

"I know you hate Liz but did you have to blow up the whole of Hemel Hempstead," he laughed.

Johnny and I had been childhood friends and I always loved his humour. But most of my friends didn't realise I was determined to solve this mystery and I didn't consider it a joke. I had to find this ex-copper and ask him why he wrote a false crime report. My quest to become a private investigator involved getting some equipment, not as sophisticated as a James Bond device, but something to help me collect evidence. I went to a shop in Kilburn that specialises in surveillance equipment and bought a recording device to hide in the lining of my suit jacket. I persuaded my son, Caolan to operate my video camera and film the conversation, if and when I spoke with ex-copper Hughes. I thought it best to record our meeting in case Hughes made false allegations afterwards.

It was a sunny Sunday in July as we drove to Luton in the borrowed 4x4, with tinted windows. We arrived just after five that evening and parked outside Hughes's house. "Camera rolling, tape machine on and action". I walked up the gravel path and knocked on the door. A dog barked from inside the house but no one answered. I knew it was his car in the driveway because I had followed him a couple of times but it looked like there was no one at home. We drove back to the petrol station on the main road and had a coffee. We sat in the garage and I slowly resigned myself to the fact that we may have missed him and today may have been a complete waste of time. But Caolan suggested we go back and try one more time before we gave up.

As we drove into Hughes's Street again, I noticed someone unloading tools from the back of the car at number 28.

"It's him," I shouted, "quick, switch the camera on."

"Are you sure?" "Yes, that's definitely him. Now's our chance!"

My heart started palpitating. I felt excited yet nervous: that feeling an actor sometimes gets just before he steps onto the stage worried if he'll remember his lines.

"Right! Tape recorder on, camera rolling, here we go," I said.

My heart thumped heavy as I approached the man who had evicted me from my home four years earlier.

"Gordon Hughes?" I asked.

"Yes, that's me."

"I'm Peter Mahon. I don't know if you remember me?"

"No." He looked unsure and stopped what he was doing.

"...from Hemel Hempstead. You evicted me from my home. Do you remember?"

"Oh yes, I remember."

"I'm curious to know why you did it?"

"Why I did it?" he then continued to unload his car. "Because that's what the law stated mate. I was just doing my job."

"I'll tell you what the law states," I said. "It is illegal for officers to remove someone from their home without a warrant or court order."

"I was doing my job, that's all."

"So why did you tell me on the night that it was a con and you were doing it because you knew Liz?"

"I didn't say that."

"I remember distinctly you saying that," I insisted.

I suddenly realised that I was standing with my back to the camera so I manoeuvred myself onto the front doorstep. I was now perfectly positioned between him and his front door.

"Excuse me, but I think you're raving mad," he shouted. "There's something wrong with you, you're nuts. Please leave my property or I will call the police."

"I don't care if you call the police..."

"Just go," he insisted.

"...wouldn't bother me." And then I smiled.

"I don't know what your problem is."

"I was made homeless because of your action."

"I'm sorry, but I was doing my job. That's all."

Hughes was still standing at the rear of his car which was behind a great big bush in the drive. I now realised that he couldn't be seen by the camera. Maybe if I encouraged him to stop unloading he'd move forward and into the camera's view.

"And why did you state I was shouting and swearing in the crime report?"

"I didn't write any crime report."

"So you didn't write that?"

"Look, wait a minute."

"Yes or no," I persisted, "Did you write that?"

"Are you going to let me answer?"

"So who wrote the crime report that said I was shouting and swearing at the officers?"

"I've got no idea. I don't write crime logs. If someone else wrote shouting and swearing, I don't know who the hell it was."

This was an interesting piece of information. If he was telling the truth, then more than one person was involved in this criminal act.

"The same week the investigation started you resigned."

"That had nothing to do with you at all," he claimed. "I had no idea you were even being... getting investigated. This is what the police are like, you know. If you want to find out what the police is really like I'll tell you."

He stopped unloading the tools and turned to face me.

"There's a book you should read and it's called, *Wasting Police Time* by a guy called PC... it was a made up name he had, and that will explain exactly why I left the police."

"So you're suggesting I buy a book by an author, whose name you can't remember, read it and that will tell me why you left the police?"

"Yes. It will explain the reasons why I left. I've done 10 years in the job, you know. I had previous service."

"...and two complaints against you. You left because you were told to leave, not because you read a book."

"Complaints mean nothing. I was doing my job," he said.

"If that's the way you do your job, I'm glad you left."

"I left the police a long time ago and I'm not interested in them or their problems." He continued, "I walked out and said fuck you, stick it up your backside and I left."

"The police have now admitted that what you did was unlawful," I told him.

"I don't know; they haven't told me anything. They didn't speak to me when I left; they haven't spoken to me since."

Even though he appeared bitter towards the police, he was not going to admit that he had done something wrong. He then suddenly said he had to go to take his wife out. I felt he had told me some of what I wanted to know so we parted, both of us politely saying goodbye. I thanked him for his time and as I drove off I felt a great relief, like a millstone had been removed from around my neck.

"Let's see what the police have to say now!" I said to Caolan.

Through my new solicitor, Tim King, a meeting was arranged with Mrs Grundy (the Legal Services solicitor) and DI Fantom, writer of a new report that tried to explain why my eviction had happened without anyone admitting guilt.

"Why do all these people in the police have funny names?" I asked Simon when I spoke to him about the meeting. "First Mr How and now Mr Fantom."

"Because they're all a bunch of wankers," he replied.

I was hoping the meeting would be an opportunity to present my new evidence but instead it turned out to be as productive as a broken down washing machine. I had spoken to Mrs Grundy on the phone a few times before, in 2005 and her abrupt manner and bad attitude gave me the image of a thin, pale, dark haired woman too mean to eat. That image couldn't have been more wrong when a fat, red-faced, blonde woman with swollen feet struggled into Tim King's office, out of breath and out of sorts. I pulled out a tape recorder from my briefcase but she immediately said she would not allow any recording of the meeting.

I had a back-up recorder hidden in my jacket. Unfortunately, when I checked it later, I discovered the thing hadn't worked so there was no evidence of what was said. She tried to get me to sign some document about secrecy but I refused point blank to sign. Then she started the meeting by stating that there would be no prosecutions of anyone and continued talking with an arrogant tone that reminded me of a school teacher who ruled by the cane. Suddenly she accused me of "not being one hundred per cent innocent in this matter." I let out a gasping. "What did you just say?" and Tim King challenged her on that point. Then she reminded me that I had had a non-molestation order against me. Mr King pointed out that it had been quashed and it was made without me being present in the court. I told her it had been falsely applied for by Mr Palfrey. She said nothing. I sat looking at her and wondered if she already knew that I had registered a complaint to the Independent Police Complaints Commission about her and the cover-ups and her unprofessional attitude. Silence hit the room when I announced that I had spoken to ex-PC Hughes. It soon became clear that this meeting with Mrs Grundy was like chewing water, pointless. It ended with nothing being achieved and an unhappy Mrs Grundy leaving with a sour face.

A week after the meeting, Tim King phoned to inform me that Mrs Grundy was threatening to pursue action for defamation if I persisted with my complaint to the IPCC about her conduct.

"Yes please," I told Mr King, "let her sue and that will give me the opportunity to present evidence of her corruption."

"It could cost you a lot of money if you lose," he advised.

"I'll take that chance," I said with a determination in my voice. "Tell Mrs Alison Grundy I'm not doing this for money. If she is allowed to do this to me then she could do it to someone else."

I didn't receive any further correspondence from Alison Grundy and neither did my solicitor and there were no new threats made from her to sue me. One month later she was replaced and was under investigation by the same people she worked for. Of course their investigation was bias and they refused to look at all the evidence I had, claiming they had dispensation from the IPCC not to look at certain letters or statements which contained accusations written by Mrs Grundy. But their claim of dispensation was not true because I had a letter from the IPCC that proved they had never granted dispensation about anything relating to Mrs Grundy. Yet the police still insisted they had been given dispensation. When I asked for a copy of the so-called letter that granted dispensation, the police insisted I could not see it because the Freedom of

Information Act prevented it being released. I never did see the letter so all I can say is, does this letter actually exist?

I said to Mr King, "Who the hell is the running the police and policing the people who police the police?"

He didn't reply.

HERTFORDSHIRE
CONSTABULARY

Mr Peter Mahon

██████████
██████████
██

Date:	25th January 2007
Our Ref:	Mahon
Your Ref:	CO 18191 2006
Contact:	Mrs A Grundy
Direct Line:	01707 354175
Direct Fax:	01707 354518
E-mail:	

Dear Sir

Re: Yourself v Independent Police Complaints Commission and 2. The Chief Constable of the Hertfordshire Constabulary
High Court of Justice – Ref: CO18191/2006

Further to our letter fo the 22nd January 2007 we are now able to tell you that your allegations against Ms Keenan have been referred to the Area Command Team for the relevant Area.

We have been informed that there will not be an investigation into your allegations. The reasons for not pursuing a criminal investigation are two fold, firstly, it is unusual for mutual allegations in domestic type disputes to be investigated in these circumstances and secondly, wasting police time is an offence rarely prosecuted as it requires the permission of the Director of Public Prosecutions and to prosecute for this offence will deter people from reporting matters to the police.

Whilst we appreciate that the above information may not be to your liking we felt it was necessary to clarify why your allegations will not be investigated.

Yours faithfully

A | G — dy

Mrs Allison Grundy
Solicitor, Legal Services

7.   'Refusal to investigate'.

CHAPTER 14

◇◇◇◇◇

How Can I Go Forward?

"You're not still suing the police?" said Jim Bradford, my musician friend who had introduced me to Simon Groom back in 2005, who became one of my greatest allies. It was now 2009; five years and it appeared to everybody, except me of course, that I was getting nowhere. The police were still defending the actions of the two officers claiming they had prevented a domestic violent situation. Why was the establishment defending Liz's account of what happened? "The system is corrupt," said Jim and he seemed to be talking sense about the way the process is set up to make it as hard as possible or even stop the common person getting justice. His words were just a reminder of what an impossible task it had become, taking on the mighty force of the police authorities. The system doesn't allow the truth to come out. Friends were suggesting that I was crawling down that dark alleyway of revenge, but what appeared obvious to them was not what I was intending. I was trying to run up that long road to justice. If the police could do this to me then they could do it to anyone and I felt, they must be exposed.

The loneliness of complaining was sometimes harder to face than the friends who told me to give up.

Telling my story was boring a lot of people to the point they were going into zombie-like trances but I couldn't stop myself. Every now and again while I was repeating my story someone would interrupt and say, "I know who you should talk to," and my first thought would be: "Oh no, not another suggestion to see a psychiatrist." But sometimes their suggestions would be an idea I had never thought of and would lead to another piece of useful information. One such suggestion was to speak to Leslie Naylor author of the book *Judge For Yourself* and she turned out to be very helpful and told me to start with the old fashion letter writing.

So I wrote to the Home Office Minister – not interested. I wrote to the Minister for Constitutional Affairs – not interested and I wrote to the Chief Superintendent of Hertfordshire Constabulary – not interested. I even wrote to Prime Minister Tony Blair's wife, who is a barrister, but she too was not interested. I was finding that the judicial system was not driven by a need to find out the truth; it was driven by individuals' ambitions within police forces to solve complaints quickly leading to career promotion at the expense of quality investigations. In my case that appeared true when Mrs Grundy, police solicitor, who was continuously accusing me of not being innocent which was based on ex-PC Hughes's crime report, was promoted to Deputy Head of Legal Services.

Alison Grundy had continued for years to refuse to release the statements of Liz and Palfrey claiming I would need to apply to the IPCC for release. When I wrote to the IPCC, they also refused, citing the Data Protection Act sections 7 and 29. So I made a 'Subject Access Request' to the Freedom of Information Unit asking for disclosure under the Freedom of Information Act 2000 but that was also refused by quoting the Data Protection Act. I wrote to the Information Commissioner's Office (ICO) and they also refused quoting sections 7 and 29 of the Data Protection Act. Each department was repeating the same reason as another department.

I had been informed by the citizen's advice bureau (CAB) that sections 7 and 29 had been misused and misapplied. When I pointed this out to the IPCC they replied stating '*We must inform you that you will need to seek advice from the ICO.*' I wrote to the ICO again which agreed that the IPCC had gone beyond their duty under the Data Protection Act in citing sections 7 and 29; however their excuse continued by stating '*overall we consider it likely that the information you have sought access to is likely to fall outside of your right of access under the Data Protection Act.*' They suggested I ask Hertfordshire Police but then told me that I would probably be refused because of – yes you've guessed it – the Data Protection Act.

Everyone was quoting the Data Protection Act without actually quoting which section states I cannot have the statements. There is no section that explains why I was being refused access. I was being sent spinning round in circles back to where I started. Therefore, I made an application to Watford County Court for the release of the two statements. I needed to get Liz and Palfrey's statements to see what I was actually being accused of.

I discovered on the internet a book called *Civil Actions Against The Police* by Richard Clayton and Hugh Tomlinson and it advised the ordinary person on how to sue the police. I phoned the British Library to find out if they had a copy and they said yes, but because they only had one copy I would have to read it in the actual reading room at the library. I was told to bring two forms of ID and a bank statement and a credit card with proof of signature. So off I went with my documents and arrived at the library full of expectation of gaining some knowledge from this book.

The new British Library, from the outside, looked like a block of 1960s council flats but walking into the spacious courtyard at the front made it appear more palatial. When I saw a little coffee stand I thought that it looked pleasant and inviting so I promised myself a coffee later. It was a bright sunny day and I was feeling relaxed, now that I was away from the intensity of my computer writing statements and letters to people that never replied. The interior of the library was in a stunning bright marble and looked really impressive. It appears they have spent millions of pounds on the interiors and just a couple of quid on the exterior. I climbed the grand marble stairs to the department that lent books. I was told to fill out an application form on a computer and then wait for 20 minutes to be called and interviewed. It all seemed a bit over the top and bureaucratic just to look at a book but if that's what I had to do, then I'd do it. Then my name was called out and the girl who interviewed me asked the same questions that I had already answered on the computer form. She then asked for proof of address and I handed her my bank statement.

"I can't accept this," she said.

"Why not?" I asked.

"It's a printout from your computer."

"And what's wrong with that?" I said.

"I need to see the original statement."

I tried to explain that the bank had stopped sending paper statements because of the new save paper policy but she insisted that she needed the original statement otherwise I would not be allowed to look at the book. I asked to see the manager and when he arrived he told me the same. Even though I had my passport, my driving licence, my debit and credit cards and my non-acceptable bank statement, they said it was not enough.

I was starting to wonder what sort of book this was, top secret or rare. Maybe the police had warned the library not to give Peter Mahon 'that book'! I offered to let someone watch me while I read the book but the manager said that would infringe my Human Rights. Isn't it ironic, I was trying to find some information about the police abusing my Human Rights and the library manager was refusing to watch me read in case it infringed my Human Rights? I left the place so disgusted that I didn't even stop for the coffee that I had promised myself earlier.

I went to the Barbican library and they said they could order the book for me with no restrictions and to my surprise they told me it would be ordered from the British Library. I was disappointed though when I went to collect the book, one month later, and noticed it had been loaned from Lancaster University instead. Maybe the British Librarians couldn't bring themselves to part with it. I was given the book with no conditions or limitations and took it home to read. Winston Churchill once said, *"the secret of success is going from failure to failure without losing enthusiasm."* It was easy for him to say that because he had an army. I was just one man drowning in a bath of legal difficulties against an unsympathetic judicial system.

I looked through the book for days photocopying sections that related to my problem and the more I read the more I realised I needed another solicitor, one who specialises in 'action against the police.' But it was not as easy as it sounded. I had been phoning solicitors for years who were listed as dealing with police matters and not one of them thought my case was worth fighting. I hadn't been arrested, I hadn't been charged and the claim for infringement of my Human Rights had now run out of time. "You can only claim breach of your Human Rights within one year after the incident," said all the solicitors. I started to realise it wasn't the amount of evidence I had, it was basically down to the amount of money I was prepared to pay or the amount of money legal aid thought I possibly could be awarded.

It took six months for Tim King's application for legal aid to be considered and when I won permission for a Judicial Review against the IPCC in the Royal Courts of Justice, that's when legal aid accepted my application for funding to sue Hertfordshire Constabulary. I felt I was in with a fighting chance. I now had the backing of legal aid. But time dragged on and it took another year before a meeting with the big city barrister was arranged. He was the man who had told me I had a good case for receiving an out of court settlement.

"I'm not really interested in settling out of court," I said, "I want to get into court to expose the corruption."

Mr King and the big city barrister looked at each other and said nothing.

When I went home I looked up the big city barrister's name on the internet and checked his CV. I didn't know what to think when I dis-covered he specialised in defending police officers who had allegations made against them. Why did Tim King introduce me to him? Surely my case would be a conflict of interest to this big city barrister.

Weeks turned into months and it took an unusually long time, but even-tually my application to Watford County Court to get permission for the release of the two statements made by Liz and Palfrey had been granted a hearing date. I had applied for the statements long before my solicitor, Mr King had been involved. Mrs Grundy (police's solicitor) had refused for over three years to disclose the contents of the statements and I was still unsure what Liz and her brother were accusing me of. I turned up at court with my loyal supporters Simon, Jenna and Masako but Mr King and my big city barrister didn't show up. Instead a replacement barrister was sent. He told me my hearing had been cancelled. "What!" I stood there wondering if I should scream or just lie down on the floor and cry. Apparently Tim King and Alison Grundy had decided, without my knowledge, that the hearing should be adjourned. No one had asked me and I was the person who had applied for the hearing.

"I didn't tell Mister King to adjourn."

"Well, that's something you'll have to take up with him," the stand-in barrister said. "There's nothing I can do now that the other side have agreed to the adjournment."

I immediately told him to go into court and explain that it was not I who cancelled the hearing but he said he would be 'professionally embarrassed' to ask the judge to consider this application after it had been agreed by both parties to be adjourned. I could feel my face getting hotter and hotter. I was now getting angry but Simon, who always appeared angry to me, reminded me not to get too heated because I needed to stay calm to go in front of the judge. I told the stand-in barrister to go into court and fight for my case as if his life depended on it. He refused.

"Are you resigning then?" I said.

"You don't have a chance in hell in getting these statements today."

"I will go into court myself then," I insisted.

"You can't do that," he said.

"Well, I'm not happy about this" I said, "you have been paid and you should be working for me."

He stayed silent. I could see in his face he was baffled.

"I'm going to have to phone your solicitor." And he left the room.

He returned and said he could not represent me because he would not be allowed but was willing to go into court and explain the situation to the judge, and then he would stand at the back of the court while I presented my case. I agreed and we went into court.

The room was small, not like the normal sized courts I had seen before.

It was just a room with one big desk and a large tape recorder in front of the judge. The stand-in barrister stood in front of the desk. The judge, a woman who looked stern and grumpy, sat glaring at everyone. I sat beside the barrister and Simon, Jenna and Masako sat near the doorway.

"Who are all these people?" the judge grumbled.

Simon started to speak when the judge interrupted.

"Are you a solicitor?"

And before he replied I asked if I could speak.

"If you plead your case now it will fall on deaf ears," she said.

How could I plead my innocence when I was told not to speak? I sat there feeling betrayed by my legal team, in front of a judge who was refusing to talk to me like a spoilt child. There was also confusion about the paperwork. My first application to the court had been sent back to me and this was the version the judge had. The second amended application was the version the stand-in barrister had and no one really knew which version the police had. What a mess. It was a total catastrophe. The plan that the barrister and I had agreed was now abandoned but the stand-in barrister did put up a good argument and between him and the judge they decided the best course was to set another date for a hearing. We were offered a date in March.

"Is that enough time for the other side to respond?" asked the judge.

I whispered to the barrister that they had already had five years to respond and now they have a couple of months surely that's time enough. He agreed and said I had a point. The judge agreed and we were granted the 30 March 2009.

I left that court realising that Tim King and Mrs Alison Grundy had been communicating with each other and had made an agreement without consulting me first.

"Give him a fuckin' rollicking," said Simon.

But I knew that would not achieve what I wanted. I was in a bit of a dilemma. If I shout at Mr King, he will cancel my legal aid funding. I can't sack him and I also can't trust him and I knew it would be impossible to find another solicitor willing to help me to apply for legal aid. As for my big city barrister, I definitely needed to get rid of him but I didn't want to take on another court case suing my solicitor for malpractice with all the headaches I was suffering trying to sue the police.

Leslie Naylor had suggested I write to Mike Mansfield QC who had a reputation of taking on difficult cases like 'the Guildford four' and 'the Birmingham six' but would he feel my case was big enough? After all, 'the Hemel Hempstead one' was not going to make front page headlines.

I wrote a letter and told Mr Mansfield I had never been in trouble with the police except for that time I was charged with riding a bicycle with no lights. When I went to court I pleaded guilty but insane. I thought humour might get my letter noticed but in afterthought it was not necessary and was a really stupid idea. He did reply but said he was too busy promoting his book around the country and anyway, I needed to have a solicitor to instruct Mr Mansfield as only certain barristers can be approached directly. When I suggested to Tim King we should approach Mr Mansfield, he dismissed it as a fool-hardy idea and would find it impossible to justify to the legal aid funding such a high profile barrister with a high fee. Mr King seemed to object to every suggestion I made. I decided to confront him and see what he had to say about why he cancelled my hearing without consulting me?

As for the big city barrister I wrote to him pointing out all the mistakes he had made in his argument about my evidence. He replied saying he would write a new advice statement. But that turned out to be worse than his original advice. His statement was so one-sided in favour of the police I would be stupid to use him to defend me.

I phoned Tim King but I resisted going into attack mode. We discussed having a meeting because I wanted to confront him face to face. I asked him if it would be possible to have the stand-in barrister representing me when I return to court for the release of Liz and Palfrey's statements. He said he would ask him. As our conversation progressed he started admitting that he and my big city barrister were reluctant to go to court.

"The legal aid funding will not consider it to be a strong enough case to justify the cost of a hearing to acquire Liz and Palfrey's statements," he said.

"Do you know how angry and embarrassed I was, turning up at the court not knowing the hearing had been cancelled?" I blurted out.

"I thought it was understood when I phoned you on Friday..." he tried to explain but I interrupted.

"...let me remind you that you said you were considering adjournment and I said 'no way' would I agree. I also told you we could discuss it on Monday morning at court."

There was silence. I didn't want to get angry but it was hard not to. I told him I had seen the paperwork in court. I knew that he and Alison Grundy had cancelled the hearing Friday lunch time and he had not phoned me until 6pm Friday evening. I didn't actually accuse him of deceit but I'm sure he knew that's what I was insinuating.

"Um... well, all I can do is apologise and assure you that there has been no underhandedness or collusion going on between me and Mrs Grundy."

"Oh yes?"

"It's not that your barrister doesn't want to go to court, it's simply that the amount of money required would not justify a hearing," said Mr King.

That's when I realised that he and my barrister had not been straight with me and had been stringing me along for years while all the time never having any intention of taking the police all the way to court. I told him not to make any future decisions without consulting me first and hung up.

I was now raging. I had been deceived for years and it looked like they had only taken on my case to fill their own pockets. I just didn't know who to trust anymore and with people like that on my side, how on earth was I expected to win against the police? As John Lennon sang, *"How can I go forward when I don't know which way I'm facing?"*

CHAPTER 15

◇◇◇◇◇

Lawrence Was Just
What I Needed

There was heavy snow all over London in February 2009 so I was forced to cancel everything including a meeting with Masako's solicitor. There was a small chance that her solicitor would take on my case but that turned out to be another dead end. Transport had ground to a halt but I struggled through the slush to King's Cross station to buy a copy of *The Big Issue* magazine. I had been interviewed by one of their journalists, Michael Parker, a month or so earlier to tell my story. To my surprise it had a full page report with a full size photograph opposite. I didn't expect the article to be a main feature. I looked bloody awful in the photograph, like a fugitive from a war zone but the article was well constructed and focused on the many thousands of complaints the police receive while few are upheld. The article reported on a system that is failing to police the police. *The Big Issue* seller didn't seem to have many customers because of the snow and the streets of London appeared deserted on that cold February night. I went to show the magazine to Jenna but she had also bought a couple of copies as keepsakes.

"I'm very proud of you for still fighting dad," she smiled and gave me a big hug. "I'm going to tell all my friends and put this on my Facebook."

I left message after message at Tim King's office but he didn't reply. A lot of people didn't go to work because of the snow so maybe that was the reason. Eventually, a few days later, he returned my call and we arranged a meeting for 16 February. As I travelled in the car to the meeting I heard on the radio that the Crown Prosecution Services (CPS) had decided that no officer would be prosecuted in the Charles de Menezes shooting in London. Well, I thought, if the police can get away with killing someone who is totally innocent then no one will be brought to justice in my matter.

I walked into Tim King's office and I wasn't sure how he was going to react to my request to find a new barrister or how he would react to me. Had he been deceitful or did he just assume that I would go along with whatever he said? He told me he had spoken to the stand-in barrister but the barrister had cordially refused to represent me. He again claimed he thought that I was fully aware and understood what was happening about my case. I told him I was aware of what I wanted to happen but not aware of what he decided would happen. We discussed my case for nearly two hours and he told me that my barrister had written a new advice that stated I had a very weak case and should not go to court. This was not quite the same opinion he had given in his original advice four years earlier. The barrister was now predicting that I would only receive about £500 and Legal Aid will not fund a case of such low quantum. He also said I should not waste my own money on a private prosecution. The big city barrister's advice finished by saying, *"In my view, the claim is not one where public funding should be continued; therefore, I will be telling Legal Aid Services to stop the funding."* I assumed, because I had requested the stand-in barrister to replace him, that he might be slightly peeved by that but I didn't expect him to cancel my legal aid funding.

I phoned the Legal Aid Services but they told me I had no control whether I received legal aid or not, it was down to my barrister. Tim King informed me that he would send a 'letter of claim' to the police and when I receive a response I would have to make a decision about whom my barrister would be. If I didn't get a *pro bono* barrister, then I would have to get a privately funded one.

Once again I applied to CAB for a *pro bono* barrister. This time a female barrister, whom I never actually got to meet, was appointed to my case. Unfortunately, she agreed with the opinion of my big city barrister that damages would very unlikely be awarded. I was starting to wonder if the whole legal establishment was trying to stop me suing the police and I had become the crazy person everyone said I was. The case has been delayed, diverted, mishandled, forgotten, abandoned and now concluded. I was starting to think that maybe I should give up. If at first you don't succeed, give up! That's all I've heard for the past seven years and I have had enough. I now wanted to push the button to stop the world? The female barrister also advised me to have another meeting with Hertfordshire police and take whatever money they offer. To me that was not a solution. I wanted justice. A false crime report had been made and I wanted some kind of rectitude, apology and a prosecution. And Mr King was now saying he would be unable to attend any such meeting with Hertfordshire police.

"If you're not doing this for money, why bother?" he said.

"Well, would you be interested in representing me if I paid you?" I asked.

At first he said yes and then a week later he said no. I didn't know what to make of that. He emphasised that I will not get the amount of money I expect and I may even lose my flat in east London.

"Well, I don't care," I said, "If I lose this case I will tell the judge to send me to prison immediately because I will never pay any money to the police."

Mr King and I said our goodbyes and parted. I was now without a barrister and solicitor - again.

I went straight back onto the telephone calling every solicitor I could find who dealt with 'action against the police'. When I told them what I had achieved, some showed a little interest, some were shocked, some even asked for my files to assess the case but once again no one thought the matter was worth pursuing.

It was November 2009 when I eventually found a firm called Doves who had an office on the Old Kent Road tucked away in a basement. The Nigerian solicitor, whose name I could never pronounce, invited me in to discuss the matter. When I went for the first time to meet him, his receptionist was uncertain who I was meant to see because she didn't understand my mispronunciation of the solicitor's name and I couldn't really grasp what she was saying. I think it was also her first day because she didn't really have a clue who was who and what was what. She kept picking up the phone telling people to wait. She must have had a dozen callers hanging on. I discovered after a few visits to Doves offices that they had a different receptionist every week, if not every day and every one of them was a trainee. Every solicitor I meet has a messy office, piles of papers everywhere and total disorder and this solicitor was no different. We sat and he listened to my story, even though he didn't understand a lot of what I was saying we both repeated each sentence two or three times. He couldn't understand my Northern Irish accent and I also couldn't understand his strong Nigerian accent but we struggled on.

I told him about the investigations I had made and the evidence I had gathered over the years.

"Are you a journalist?" he asked.

I took that as a compliment. He must have thought I had done a lot of research and of course I had. He then asked me if I was going to go for legal aid or privately funded. I told him I had already had legal aid and it would be impossible to be granted it again therefore I had no other option than to go for privately funded. On that note he immediately said he would take on my case and then asked for a £500 deposit. I felt a bit uneasy at parting with my money before any letters or telephone calls were made but there was no one else I could ask for help; it was either him or nobody.

The first thing he did was ask for my files from my previous solicitor, Tim King and when after a couple months the papers still hadn't arrived, he threatened to report him to the Solicitors Regulation Authority. I was impressed with his aggressive approach but also confused why Mr King was hesitating and reluctant to release all my documents.

We decided, well I decided to do it, was have a conference with a top QC who was knowledgeable and experienced in police matters. The Nigerian solicitor sent a young solicitor to accompany me, who was also Nigerian and he had an even stronger accent. At first I was reluctant to let this solicitor; whose name was Lawrence, come to the meeting because I had to pay his hourly rate of £150. With the QC charging me £2500 just to sit and tell me what the police could do and what I can't do, I was unwilling to spend more money for a young solicitor to sit and listen. I felt he should be paying me for the experience.

We went into a big office in the Doughty Street chambers and took our positions round the large mahogany conference table with its complimentary jugs of water scattered along the centre. I asked if I could record the meeting and the QC said she had no objections, even though she thought it was unusual. If we were going to sit talking for three hours, I needed a recording of the conversation in case I missed or forgot an important point of law. It was also cheaper than paying the QC extra money to write a summary of the meeting. And just like a comedy film, when I switched on my recorder, a workman, directly outside the open window started cutting with a grinder through stone slabs. Normally I would have found it funny but this was too serious to laugh about. I could hardly hear the QC but she carried on talking as if nothing was happening. It could have been gobbledegook for all I could hear but between the intense noisy bits, when I assume the workman was having tea breaks, I got the opportunity to ask questions. She told me what the police can do, will do and won't do but she didn't tell me what I can do or maybe she had said that bit when I couldn't hear. Lawrence turned out to be the kind of solicitor I needed and wanted. He did everything I suggested whereas Mr King had always boohooed every tactic I wanted to try.

As the months went by I realised I now had a solicitor who agreed with the way I wanted to fight the police and it looked like we would be having a hearing by January 2012.

Now that I had a solicitor the police requested a meeting but only with Lawrence, emphasising that I should not be present. Lawrence phoned me to ask what he should do. I was impressed that he was conferring with me.

"Tell them we will agree to a meeting but only if I can be present and the meeting can be recorded."

Lawrence did exactly what I requested and we waited. The police never replied.

The pressure was easing on me and I felt a great relief that I now had someone on my side. I could at last see that my case was looking a little less opaque. I took a driving job so I could pay Doves solicitors and worked 12 hour days to earn as much money as possible to pay the massive legal fees. Working was also helping me cope with the stress and helped me feel better about myself.

Things were moving pretty well until 27 September 2011 when a letter popped through my letterbox. Dove's solicitors were closing down and would cease practising from 30 September. I couldn't believe it. I was a couple of months away from going to court and I now had no legal team. Simon told me to represent myself in court but I didn't feel confident enough after my disastrous appearance in the High Courts in 2007 when I lost my first hearing against the IPCC. It felt like 'ground hog day' having to phone solicitors again trying to persuade them it was worth taking the police to court. None of them were interested so it looked like I was going to lose without even having a chance to fight.

After spending seven years and approximately £20,000 the battle was now over. I was not going to get my day in court.

I went to Watford County Court and handed in a letter asking for an extension of time as I had no solicitor or barrister to continue with my case. I was asked to fill in an application notice form in triplicate but there was no guarantee that the Judge would agree to the request. I then drove to Doves solicitors in south London to collect all my files. I was kept waiting for hours because there was no one there who could find my documents. I was not going to leave without my papers then the Nigerian solicitor whose name I never could pronounce, strolled into the office like a tourist wandering through Madam Tussauds. He was looking through piles of papers while I sat there watching him and eventually he came over to me and apologised for the collapse of the practice. He claimed their insurance premium was too high and so they were forced to close down. By the time I left Doves offices at around four o'clock, I was really hungry and I still didn't have any of my files. I had been driving all day from my home in east London to Watford and then back through London to the Old Kent Road and hadn't had the opportunity to stop and eat. I went to a nearby shop and bought what looked like a healthy wholemeal Mexican chicken sandwich. But later that evening I threw it back up. I spent the next three days in bed with food poisoning. Things couldn't get any worse...could they?

CHAPTER 16

◇◇◇◇◇

ANYONE THERE?

My Nigerian solicitor had assured me that Lawrence would continue with my case when he started his new job with Goldfields solicitors in Plumstead, south London.

"You have a very strong case and Lawrence will continue working on it," he said.

I wasn't feeling confident with those words because I had been promised so much by so many for so long and none of it had materialised. So I walked away thinking "I'll believe that when I see it." Weeks went by and Lawrence wasn't replying to any of my emails and of course Doves solicitors' phones were not being answered. So I started my search for a new solicitor again. Even though I didn't feel I had the energy to pursue another barrage of rejections, my stubbornness and determination refused to allow me to give up.

I wrote to Goldfields solicitors trying to establish whether or not Lawrence was joining their practice or whether they had another solicitor who might be adventurous enough to take on my claim. Meanwhile deadline dates were being missed and requests from the police for my medical records to be sent to a psychiatrist hadn't happened. Lawrence had included in my claim costs for Post-Traumatic Stress therefore my medical records had to be examined. The ironic fact was that a solicitor could request the release of my medical records a lot easier than if I asked for them myself. I had visions of police solicitors all sitting round a table with tea and biscuits rubbing their hands with glee because I was now without legal representation. My thoughts were in overdrive and I imagined the police laughing, "Let's go down the pub because that loony Mahon doesn't stand a chance without a solicitor." I never received a reply to my letter from Goldfields so I decided to go to their office and find out what was happening. I drove up and down Plumstead High Street looking for a sign saying Goldfields or even solicitors but without success. I found number 54 but it wasn't a solicitor's office, it was an estate agent. I decided to go in and make enquiries. There was a young girl sitting behind a desk filing her nails.

"Did this use to be a solicitor's office, Goldfields?" I asked.

"Still is," she replied, "their office is through that door at the back."

She pointed to a little white door at the back of the shop but I couldn't see any signs and there wasn't a clue to what was beyond the door. Could it be a dungeon or a brothel or even worse – a scrap yard with a pile of useless solicitors waiting for a mug like me? It came as a big surprise when I stepped into a very plush reception area with various offices leading off it. But nobody was about.

"Hello," I called out as I walked around but no one answered.

"Is there anybody there?" But still no reply. I peeped into one of the offices. It was very clean and tidy, not the usual mess I've experienced in other solicitor's places.

"HELLO," I shouted but still no reply.

I went back out into the shop to ask the girl where everybody was but she was now busy. There were two couples making enquiries about properties. I felt like I was stepping in and out of Doctor Who's Tardis. From the outside it appeared to be a small shop but behind that small door was a large reception area with a complex of offices. I stepped back into the Tardis and stood at the desk silently observing. I then heard a voice coming from one of the distant offices. Could this be a solicitor? I decided to wait and see. The door eventually opened and out walked a tall black man in a very snazzy, stylish suit.

"Can I help you?"

And I went into my spiel about the police, how I lost my solicitor and why I was there because I was told Lawrence would be working for the firm Goldfields.

"Lawrence doesn't work here," he said, and by what he told me it sounded like he never would.

He took me into one of the offices and started explaining that he was a friend of Lawrence's and he was trying to help by allowing him to use the firm's name to continue practising. It all sounded a bit dodgy but I was desperate and willing to listen in case he said what I wanted to hear. He phoned Lawrence there and then and I spoke to him on his speaker phone. Lawrence said he would start working on my case immediately. I reminded him that he said that two weeks previous and nothing had happened. I told him my GP had not been contacted by anyone in connection with my medical records being sent to the psychiatrist and he had promised that would be done. He mumbled something about not being able to contact my doctor but I was feeling now the time had come to decide whether we should part company or not. He promised faithfully to speak to my GP and would let me know what was happening, now that he's working with his new firm, OJN solicitors. After we finished the call I asked the Goldfields solicitor if he would be willing to represent me in my matter but he said they didn't have a licence to do claims against the police. I left feeling downhearted and totally confused why promises were being made and yet nothing was happening. What were they up to? I didn't know what to do. How many doors did I have to bang on before someone would hear me? I was starting to resign myself to failure and even my supporters, Maurice and Simon, were baffled as to what advice they could give.

I received another letter from Mike Penning MP because he was trying to help me arrange an interview with the Right Hon. Nick Herbert MP (Minister of State for Policing at the Home Office) but the Policing Minister was not responding to our request for a meeting. Mr Penning agreed with me that police authorities should hold officers to account when they step out of line but it appears that officers are allowed to resign and are never investigated for their actions. We tried for months to get a meeting with Mr Herbert at the Home Office without success. I was beginning to think I would have a better chance if I asked the Queen for a date. I tried to phone Doves again and to my surprise the Nigerian solicitor answered. I asked him for my files. He said he would speak to Lawrence and I said "No, I want my file." He assured me that it would be no problem but he needed to speak to Lawrence. I told him that I had spoken to Lawrence and nothing was happening. "I want my files," I insisted.

He said, "Let me speak to Lawrence first."

"I want my files." I said, "I have paid you a lot of money and I want my files."

He told me I would not find a solicitor now so close to the trial. I told him I would need my files to find another solicitor. He promised to phone me back as soon as he spoke to Lawrence. He didn't phone back and neither did Lawrence. Out of desperation I decided to phone a solicitor that my friend Jim Fitzgerald recommended as someone who could help. Jim scribbled two numbers on a piece of paper.

"One is his office number but you've a better chance of getting him on his mobile," said Jim.

"These numbers are very long, where is he?" I asked.

"Athens."

"What!" I shouted, "Why the hell would I phone a solicitor in Athens?"

"Because you're fuckin' desperate."

God only knows why Jim thought a solicitor in Greece would be able to help me but Jim was a bit drunk when he recommended him. I wasn't sure if it was a stupid idea or not but then everyone had told me it was a stupid idea to sue the police in the first place. So I phoned the solicitor in Athens. He was a bit surprised that I was phoning from London but told me he would try to think of someone who could help and let me know. We never spoke again.

The weeks were flying by and nothing was happening then out of the blue Lawrence phoned and offered to continue representing me. The new firm he had joined agreed to allow him to continue with my case and he admitted feeling guilty about abandoning me so close to the trial date. I told him I would think about it and let him know and then I put the phone down. What was I doing? I didn't have any other solicitor interested so who was I fooling? I wasn't convinced about Lawrence after the way Doves had messed me around. Could I trust him? Could I trust anybody? It was trusting Liz that got me into this mess and this whole affair had caused me to distrust the police, solicitors, barristers and everyone. I was even starting to doubt myself. Could I stay cool under the relentless pressure of being let down by so many so called professionals? I was angry on the inside but trying to look calm on the outside. I wanted to throw paint over Liz's car. I wanted to stand outside Hemel Police station demonstrating and I wanted to protest outside Hughes house exposing a corrupt officer. But thank God I listened to my common sense and decided that was not the way to get justice.

After much discussion and lots of debating with my supporters and friends, I decided to phone Lawrence and ask him to represent me again. When I phoned, he told me he would get my files from Doves and continue with my case. I was very nervous because I was frightened he would do something behind my back without consulting me first. But he immediately arranged a meeting with the psychiatrist and a barrister and applied to Watford County Court for permission to continue with my case. We asked for a new trial date. I was hoping and praying that things were back under control.

CHAPTER 17

◇◇◇◇◇

Do Not Adjust Your Head

Everything was up and running again. I had Lawrence back, even though I was a bit sceptical, but I felt I had no other option but to trust him. I also had a barrister, though I hadn't met her yet so things seemed to be back on track.

As for the police, I suppose the vast majority of officers deserve commendation and gratitude but it is difficult to overstate the seriousness of a situation that I did not look for or want. I discovered that police culture is unduly secretive and inclined to prioritise the protection of its own. For the average citizen, if it's your word against a police officer, you will almost certainly lose. No one believed me and that was so frustrating. It drove me mad. The officers whom I had to deal with, had less knowledge of the judicial system than my next-door neighbour's cat and legal professionals were telling me that the police delaying and misquoting the law was deliberate. All I knew was the whole matter had dragged on for far too long and it was pushing me into a deep, dark place and that's what the police try to do. I was clinging to the edge of sanity. Am I crazy to want justice? Everyone says I am. How do you know if you're crazy? According to my doctor and the psychiatrist, the police had insisted I consult, I was now officially depressed? According to other people I was ill-advised to try and take on the police. Some people laughed, some people were astonished and the majority of people thought I was foolish, even stupid to try and sue the police.

"That's good," said Lawrence.

"Is it?" I asked, "Does this not mean I'm a bit... bonkers and not to be taken seriously?"

"No no! This psychiatrist's report proves that what the police have been doing over the past seven… eight years has affected your mental health. The report is in our favour."

"Oh!"

My meeting with the psychiatrist, a happy little Indian man, was decided in conjunction with my solicitor and Hertfordshire police to determine whether or not I have been mentally scarred by the actions of the police.

"I hope you don't mind me asking," I stuttered, trying to be simultaneously blunt and diplomatic, "how can you, as a psychiatrist, tell me about my mental health?"

He sat back in his big leather chair, his teeth dazzling white as his grin swung from ear to ear like a skipping rope.

"You are quite right Mr Mahon and to be perfectly honest with you, it's practically impossible to tell in just one interview so I will need to meet with you again once or maybe twice to talk about how the whole thing affected you and when you became depressed and for how long."

So he was going to decide if I was depressed by what I tell him. I say I'm depressed and he writes a report saying Peter Mahon is depressed. Doesn't seem very scientific to me! If I tell him I'm not sure how I feel what will he then write?

I had been very down at the beginning of all this, especially in 2005 when I first went to see my GP and he did recognise serious depression. And even though he prescribed anti-depressants, the pressure from the police and the false allegations from Liz could not be eliminated by a few tablets. Now that I had Lawrence taking a lot of the legal pressure from me, I should be feeling better. But I wasn't. I was neglecting everyday tasks that I should have been dealing with and not organising my financial affairs. Instead I had overdosed on my obsession to taking on the police.

The psychiatrist asked about my childhood, my family and had I ever been depressed before.

"No!" I sharply replied. "I get fed up now and again but never as down as I have been these last few years."

"It's a very complicated and unusual case," he smiled, staring straight into my eyes. "I usually deal with car insurance injury cases."

I told myself not to look away. I had read in a book *How To Conduct Yourself In An Interview* that the best thing to do was not to look away when the interviewer is asking a question. I was also told by some wise old man that people who don't look you straight in the eye when answering your questions are lying. I was trying hard to look him straight in the face and be serious but his big happy grin was encouraging me to smile. I was forced to look at the floor, the ceiling or the posters on the walls otherwise I would burst out laughing and that is not one of the symptoms of a depressed man. Why do I have to be interviewed by a jolly little doctor on such a serious subject or is this part of his examination technique to try and suss me out?

"Have you ever had any thoughts of suicide Mr Mahon?"

"Not really."

"What do you mean, not really?"

"Well, I do have this strong urge to get away and live on a desert island. I want to get away from people because I just don't trust them anymore."

"But no thoughts of self-harm?"

"No."

"Have you got a partner at the moment?"

"No."

He shuffled through some papers.

"I see by your doctors notes that you have been complaining of depression over the past few years."

"Well yes. I just couldn't understand that every time I produced evidence that contradicted what I was being accused of, the police would just ignore it. That's what got me down."

I continued rambling on and on about the police and how much they lied. He had started me on my journey from 2004 to the present.

"And you say you're not in a relationship at present?"

"No. I'm just not interested in women. I keep thinking about the police all the time," I said.

That may have sounded a bit weird but it was how I felt.

"I think to complete my report I will need to see you again next week," he smiled. "See my secretary and she will give you another appointment."

After an hour with him I was so glad to get out of that office. I had to restrain myself through the pressure of circumstances and a sense of obligation, not to laugh. I thought that if he writes a report concluding that I was happy then the police barrister will argue, how can this man be depressed if he's laughing? I knew inside that I was depressed because it was a more intense feeling than I had ever experienced before and I was really struggling to face each day. I had a persistent belief that if I walked around with my true feelings displayed on my face then friends and family would tell me to pull myself together. But if I walked around with an artificial smile then people would question my sanity. Was it a mistaken notion I had? I tried very hard to be jovial on the surface but inside I was painfully unhappy.

My second meeting with the psychiatrist was at the same place, the London Independent Hospital in Stepney Green and when I walked into his office he was still smiling. I was still unsure what I was expected to say. I had never been interviewed or analysed or interrogated by someone in the medical profession before to calculate my mental health. I assumed I was normal and had a healthy mind until this whole episode with the police had cast great doubts.

"Could I ask you to keep your answers short and to the point this time?"

That was the first thing he said as I sat down. So he thinks I talk too much or he just didn't want to hear the full story again. I did tend to go on a bit.

"I've been reading your doctor's records and he has written that you are obsessed with what the police have done to you."

"Yes."

"I do understand Mr Mahon so don't feel that I'm criticizing."

"No."

"When I said keep your answers short I didn't literally mean..."

"Sorry."

"It must have been terrible to have been arrested..."

"I wasn't arrested. I was just kicked out of my home onto the street."

"You weren't arrested or charged?"

"No"

He seemed surprised at that answer. It took the smile off his face but only for a moment.

"I see," and he scribbled some notes in his pad.

After an hour of questioning, I felt ready for a drink. Going over the whole experience again was exhausting.

"Well Mr Mahon, I can see... well in my opinion from the things that you have told me over the last two meetings, I feel that you have become preoccupied with this matter and you have some residual symptoms of Post-Traumatic Stress Disorder. I would recommend eight to twelve sessions of Cognitive Behaviour Therapy."

I sat there staring at him. What am I supposed to say and what is Cognitive Behaviour Therapy?

"I anticipate a full recovery following resolution of the legal proceedings."

"Let's hope that will happen then," I said.

So now it appears that after countless efforts to petition, endless letters that went unanswered and unsuccessful requests for meetings, I have been diagnosed with 'behavioural problems'.

Lawrence wrote to Legal Services again, the solicitors who were representing the police officers, to ask for round the table talks to find a solution but that too was ignored.

I decided to write to every MP in the House of Commons, all six hundred and fifty members. It sounded foolish or even obsessive but now that I have been diagnosed as needing 'behaviour therapy', I have an excuse to behave like someone who needs therapy. Maurice helped me find the list of MPs and Masako helped by copying my letters. I wrote in my letter that there is a need to change a system that ignores police officers who perform unlawful acts and then resign to avoid being questioned. I wanted to see how many ministers would support me for a call to change the rules of the police code of conduct. I had Mike Penning MP for Hemel Hempstead on my side; all I had to do was persuade the other six hundred and forty-nine.

Masako and I sat for weeks writing letter after letter until I achieved my goal. Six hundred and forty-nine letters. I then set off like a postman on his afternoon round with the mail tucked in my bag. I arrived at Parliament Square looking for the door into the main building of the House of Commons.

"No sir, you can't come in here without an appointment."

"But I just want to deliver these letters."

"Not here sir," and he pointed in the direction of where I'd just come from. When I walked back to where I started they pointed me in the direction of somewhere else. Eventually I was sent to a place called Derby Gate off Parliament Square. I decided to disguise my accent and put on my posh voice, just in case the security officers mistook me for some kind of terrorist or mad Irishman.

"Excuse me officer, could you tell me where one could deliver some letters addressed to the members of parliament?"

"Ah afeard yer too late! Post room closed at foor-thirty."

What a surprise, the officer at the door was from Northern Ireland and had an even broader accent than myself. I couldn't change my accent now or it would look suspicious so I just mumbled a 'thank you' and walked away.

I returned a few days later and entered the security area to be greeted by a po-faced officer who looked constipated.

"Where's the letter you want to deliver?" asked the miserable looking man.

I pulled the six hundred and forty-nine letters out of my bag.

"What the... You can't deliver all those."

"Why not?"

"We can't cope with all that."

"Are you telling me that the House of Commons doesn't receive a lot of mail?"

"No, we do," he snarled, "but…You will have to put stamps on them."

"I can't afford to do that!"

"Well, we can't accept them here."

He started becoming agitated and as he walked away leaving me with the pile of letters on the counter he mumbled "no chance!" I decided to stand my ground. I was determined to complete my delivery so if he wants to remove me he will have to call the police. Maybe he should call the two officers who kicked me out of my home in Hemel. He turned round to see I hadn't moved.

"I've told you, you will have to post them."

"And what will you say to the postman who delivers them?"

"Don't get funny with me…"

Just then a sergeant walked in.

"What's going on?"

"I was just telling this gentleman that we can't accept this amount of mail."

The sergeant looked at my pile of letters.

"Nothing to do with us, that's up to them in the post room," he said.

The po-faced officer turned green with annoyance. I smiled at him and like a traffic light his face then changed to red. I took the letters through to the post room and they accepted them without any question.

Over the following weeks and months, I received 39 replies to my 649 letters with only four, possibly five because I couldn't read his handwriting, agreeing with my proposal.

I came out of that post room feeling a lot better than when I went in. But I still don't understand why some people in uniform are so unhelpful and aggressive. That officer was trying to be obstructive and he didn't even have a logical reason. I walked off, down the back streets of Westminster glad that I had written those letters and then like a vision, I saw the answer to the question that I had been battling against for the past seven years.

In big white letters on a gable wall up an alleyway someone had painted the answer. 'Do not adjust your head, reality is at fault!'

CHAPTER 18

◇◇◇◇◇

THE WOMAN WHO SWALLOWED A LIE

Liz was refusing to be a witness for the police. She was the most important witness they had and yet she declined to appear in court and the police sympathised with her decision. Her reason: she was fearful to see me again. I felt I was locked in a 'Home for the bewildered' confused why the two main witnesses, Liz and PC Hughes, were not willing to appear in court to justify their claim that I had used threatening behaviour. Why no one could see what was going on baffled me or was I baffling everyone with what I could see? Surely it was obvious that the woman and the officer had told a lie. But no one was asking why they were refusing to appear at the hearing to justify their allegations.

For the first time in my life I had borrowed thousands of pounds just to bring the police to court and I hadn't given any consideration on how I was going to pay the money back. Living on my nerves with an empty bank account and on the verge of bankruptcy, I was scared stiff that if I didn't win this case I would be ruined. And yet I had reached a point where I didn't care anymore. When I had first met Liz everyone told me she was the best thing that had ever happened to me but when I took on the police, nearly everyone told me it was the stupidest thing I had ever done. I now think the reverse. Even with all the stress and suffering I had gone through I still had a feeling of achievement because I had persevered to get my day in court. Every time I sat in my office and looked up at the little proverb that was hanging above my desk, *'if you aim for the impossible then you might just do something that's never been done before,'* I felt I still had a chance. I believed what I wanted could come true.

I arrived at Luton County Court on 21August 2012 excited but nervous, in my best suit. I had done an exploratory trip a couple of days beforehand because I wanted to find the cheapest and nearest place I could park close to the court. I had heard Luton was a difficult town for parking but I did find an open derelict space someone was renting as a low-cost car park. We made the short walk from the car park to the County Court and arrived early. I stood at the security check with my briefcase that wouldn't open trying in vain to re-set the combination number. The queue behind me was getting longer and still the damn thing refused to unlock. It was full of important papers that I hoped would prove my innocence but the combination lock wouldn't budge. The security guard stood patiently waiting while I became more and more embarrassed. This was the first time it had happened and it was the worse time to happen. Maybe that's why the briefcase was so cheap. I pushed and shoved and thumped the thing but with no success. I had to tell the security guard to let other people pass because I could see everyone in the queue was becoming agitated. Jenna started telling me off and I started panicking. I didn't know what to do. I decided to resign myself to the fact that it would never unlock again when suddenly the case burst open and all my papers fell out onto the floor.

The trial had been moved from Watford because that court apparently was too busy. Jenna and Masako came with me that first day to give support and Simon and Maurice promised to come for the following two days of the set three-day hearing.

My solicitor, Lawrence, suggested that he stay away from the court to save me money. I had never had a solicitor suggest saving me money before. I was impressed.

We waited in the reception area with all the other people who looked as anxious as I did. There was a long hallway lined with chairs and approximately six or seven court rooms off it. I was to appear in courtroom number 3 at 10.30am. Jenna and Masako sat patiently while I paced around, something I always do when I'm feeling tense and unsure.

My barrister, Ms Annard, arrived and we went into a small conference room where we talked over tactics. She was young, attractive and dressed in a dark navy suit but was softly spoken. I was concerned that she might not be heard in court and the judge would fall asleep while she was speaking. She did appear confident about the evidence we had but when she produced a last minute statement from Liz claiming '*she was petrified at the thought of seeing me again*' and stated I was '*psychologically torturing her*' that's when I became even more nervous. This new statement said I had intimidated and abused her in front of her family back in 2005 at the Watford County Court hearing; this convinced me that Liz had a problem separating fact from fiction. These claims could be easily proven false just by looking at the court transcript of that hearing in 2005 but if the judge believes this without checking then I don't stand a chance of getting justice.

Ex-PC Hughes also refused to appear in court and Mrs Grundy wasn't even called. Ms Annard said that this was beneficial to my case because the police now have a weaker defence. But I felt the whole thing wasn't being addressed seriously enough. I found out later that Liz had gone off to Norfolk on the dates the hearing was on. Was she avoiding a summons? The police had sent a female officer, Police Sergeant Karen Mellor, to Liz's house to try and persuade her to appear in court but

Liz's statement, written by the female officer, claimed that Liz was in tears 'petrified' to go anywhere near me and the hearing. Her brother Palfrey was also present at the interview and claiming the family had been 'victimised by Mahon' for over eight years. Considering I had not made any contact with Liz since December 2004, I didn't understand how they could justify that claim. The female officer even claimed that Liz's daughter Laura had also been traumatised but on second reading of the officers' statement it was clear what was really being said was that 'Laura could see that her mother was upset.' Laura was not traumatised. Liz's words were manipulated by the female officers' interpretation and designed to influence the police's biased position.

Ms Annard went off to speak to the police barrister who happened to be Buckett, the same barrister who had given me a trashing at my first appearance in the High Court back in 2007 when I represented myself against the IPCC. She returned with a smile on her face telling me the police legal team had decided to withdraw the new statement made by Liz. I felt a lot more confident now and gave a great big sigh of relief.

We all piled into the court room and I was told to sit behind my barrister. Jenna and Masako sat behind me. The police legal team had their barrister at the front accompanied by a man and a woman who sat on the same row as me. The room was big enough to keep us a good distance apart so there was no chance of having a quick peek at their notes. I looked at the opposition and wondered why they had three people and I only had one.

Okay I thought, Lawrence didn't come to court so as to save me money but why did they have two solicitors? To my surprise the young man was not a solicitor. He was PC Thurston, the other officer who had evicted me. When Adam Thurston was called, on the second day of the hearing, I was shocked when he stood up. I didn't recognise him at all but then again my eyes were half closed when we first met and it had been eight years since I had last seen Thurston under those stressful circumstances.

The clerk of the court entered and shouted "all rise" and everyone stood. Judge Kay QC walked into the courtroom wearing a black suit and smiling like a cat that had just had a bowl of cream. He didn't appear to be someone who was taking this hearing seriously but more like a theatre goer looking forward to an evening performance of a tragic comedy, which he may just find with this case.

Mr Buckett stood up and informed Judge Kay that he would not be including the new statement from Liz and then the judge announced he would not be including any evidence of Elizabeth Keenan because she had refused to attend the hearing. I wasn't sure if this was good or bad for my claim. But I discovered later, as unfamiliar as I then was with court procedure, if witnesses refuse to attend court, none of their evidence can be submitted because they are not there to swear an oath as to its truth, or present themselves for cross examination by the other side. It is a matter of justice that each side in a hearing has the right to contest the evidence submitted. With hindsight, it obviously weakened the police case because their two key witnesses had refused to appear. I also wondered with hindsight if I had asked Judge Kay to summon Liz and Hughes to court what would he have done. I now regret not telling

Ms Annard to insist that Liz and Hughes be summoned.

Ms Annard and Judge Kay consulted on the difficulties of certain statements and bundles not being received in time and she apologised to the judge because he had not received a copy of her skeleton argument in advance. But then he stated, "I have read the skeleton arguments, I have read the pleadings, I have read the witness statements and not much else. I have also looked at the conclusions of Doctor Nandy otherwise I do not think I need to look at anything else." Then he wanted to know, 'as a matter of interest', if the case was publicly funded. Ms Annard said "no." "Was it on the CFA," he asked? She again said "no." I didn't know what CFA meant but I was later told it was a way of asking if my case was 'no win no fee.' In fact, I didn't understand why he wanted to know if my case was publicly funded or not. Was that going to influence his decision? He seemed obsessed about wasting public money but showed no concerns about the public money being wasted by Hertfordshire police over the eight years defending a corrupt officer and a false crime report.

"This is a slightly complicated case in that although the main incident really occurs on one night, there is then obviously a six-year period that follows in relation to the police complaint," pleaded Ms Annard.

"In relation to aggregated features, is that really pleaded?" asked the judge.

Mr Buckett then jumped up. "No, it is not and I was going to make a point about that and perhaps I should make it now."

"I have made the point," replied the judge.

"You have," replied Buckett and then he sat down.

"He is diagnosed with suffering post-traumatic stress disorder over a considerable period of time," explained Ms Annard, "of the action that he took after 20 December was an attempt to rectify and correct the allegations that were made in relation to that night."

"Yes, well, first I do not see it really pleaded in that way," said the judge, "are we to concentrate on the events of 19 and 20 December and think about that or look at the damages in question or do we just take the whole thing in one go?"

"To a certain extent we are in your hands as to whether you would like to hear evidence in relation to everything," said Ms Annard.

The conversation about what they should discuss continued for another 15 minutes or so. Most of it was inaudible while the rest of it was beyond my understanding.

"The main complaint that is made in relation to the aggravated damages is about the passage of time," continued Ms Annard, "the complaint was not properly recorded as a complaint, so it was not properly investigated by Hertfordshire police and that has aggravated the circumstances."

"It depends under which cause of action I find," replied the judge, "and there is the medical evidence from a joint expert, which I have to say I find surprising on its face – but nevertheless it is there."

"Yes, Your Honour," agreed Ms Annard.

"Your client has some kind of post-traumatic stress, depression and dependence on alcohol as a result of the offence…" continued the judge. "Well, as a result of what? In part let us say at this stage because of what happened that night. Who could have conceived that as a result of the events of that night somebody would suffer post-traumatic stress?"

"Only in relation to the misfeasance of public office claim," said Ms Annard; "the High Court authority is quite clear that the officers have to have either known or been reckless as to whether or not their actions would cause damage that would be reasonably foreseeable. There was an immediate financial loss that night."

"That I can understand," agreed the judge, "that is the one area of damage that I can see is foreseeable. If you throw somebody out of their house, then they have to go and live somewhere else."

"And if foreseeable," said Ms Annard, "then he is entitled to claim for all of the damages that arise out of the consequences of that night."

"But this lady rings up, she is very concerned about what might happen, rightly or wrongly concerned, but she expresses her concern and to the extent that she goes to the police expressing concern, if that is the case," argued the judge.

"Mr Mahon would dispute that."

"He may well dispute it but as I understand that is not in dispute because the lady did go to the police concerned about what might happen," stated the judge. "She might be wrong about what might happen, but because of her state of mind what are the police supposed to do?"

"Well, the police have a wide range of powers available to them, but first and foremost it is a civil matter."

I immediately took a dislike to this judge and his one-sided view of how helpless Liz appeared. His point of view was not sitting comfortable with me, but what he said next really shook me to my bones.

"But what if the woman is saying I am very frightened about what is going to happen; a man is in my house… Are the police to say you have the right to go to the County Court and take out an injunction? What if he then turns around grabs a knife and kills her, what would be said then? They have taken no action and somebody has been killed."

I couldn't believe what I heard. Was this judge for real? Whose side was he on? Not mine! He had made his mind up before I had a chance to give any evidence. I immediately wanted to jump up and tell him where to stick his initial impressions. But I didn't. I just sat there looking pathetic and feeling disgusted. We're 15 minutes into the hearing and he has condemned me already. I was convinced he was going to throw the case out there and then.

"I am not saying your client would do that," said Judge Kay.

"Please, absolutely do stress that," interrupted Ms Annard.

"But the police do not know," continued the judge, "and they have taken no action and somebody has been killed".

Ms Annard tried to persuade the judge that if somebody had reported an offence and an offence had been committed then the officers could have made an arrest. She said the officers were not looking at the circumstances on that evening and therefore had no reasonable apprehension that I was about to commit a breach of the peace. She insisted they had no power to take preventative action short of arrest. She told him that the officers put me out on the street, took my keys and told me if I returned I would be arrested.

"What should they do?" asked the judge.

"He should have been arrested, if he had committed an offence," she told him.

I thought she was putting up a good argument but I felt her voice was a little bit too soft and moderate. I wanted to hear her voice being more aggressive and forceful. I felt this judge needed convincing in a stronger way.

"So they have to say we are sorry but we cannot do anything about it." Said the judge.

"The first thing I would like to say Your Honour is, I would invite you to perhaps look at the evidence…"

"You may convince me in the end that my concern is entirely wrong, but I have very real concerns about the practicality of a situation like that, where if it goes wrong the police will be sued, criticised, pilloried in the newspapers because they did not take any action. They left somebody in the house that subsequently killed someone."

I sat there listening to the judge using the word 'killed' more than once and wondered if I was at the wrong trial. Am I being accused of murder and no one has bothered to tell me yet?

"Your Honour, the police have powers; they have a huge range of powers and whenever they think that someone is physically in danger they are able to arrest a perpetrator, so the first point that I would like to make is that they have to look at the circumstances as they are."

"It is a fly and not a wasp?" asked the judge. I wasn't sure exactly what he meant.

"No, it is not a wasp," replied Ms Annard. "When you look at the actual evidence that has been given by the police officers; the statements that have been written, interviews they have given, those circumstances do not give rise to a reasonable apprehension that there was about to be an imminent breach of the peace. If they had a reasonable belief that he was about to commit a crime they could have arrested him, but they did not do that."

"They make a decision in the middle of the night, a snap decision based upon circumstances that present themselves to them," argued the judge. "They had two choices, a woman who was concerned about her safety and a man inside the property. I would have thought it is a fairly low threshold."

"To take preventative action short of arrest is actually a very high threshold," said Ms Annard.

"I am just saying that this is my initial impression," replied the judge.

"Your Honour, would you like to have an opportunity to read some of the documents that have been indicated in the chronology as being key documents or would you rather Mr Mahon was called to give evidence now?"

"Would you like me to read them: would it be a good idea?" asked the judge.

"It would provide some of the background."

"All right," agreed the judge, "I think that is a good idea."

Mr Buckett then tried to persuade the judge to read the statement from Liz dated January 2005 that related to my sources of income and also the extent of monies paid and work done by me to the property in Hemel Hempstead. But Ms Annard tried to explain that it was a series of allegation made by Liz Keenan about me inappropriately subletting my flat in London. She pointed out that I strenuously disputed Liz's claims and I had letters to prove that her accusations were simply not true. She said Buckett was trying to put in evidence that was completely irrelevant and it was just an attempt to blacken my name.

"I am capable of working out what is irrelevant," said the judge. "I will let you know when I am ready."

And the court was adjourned for a short break. I leaned forward and whispered to Ms Annard, "He's certainly not on my side."

It appeared to me that Judge Kay was defending the two police officers' actions while Mr Buckett sat waiting for the guilty verdict against me to be announced.

We all went outside to wait for the judge to read the documents.

CHAPTER 19

◇◇◇◇◇

THE TRUTH, THE WHOLE TRUTH AND NOTHING BELIEVED

The court resumed and I was the first person to be called. When I stood up to walk to the witness stand my barrister nodded to me not to take the paperwork I was about to grab from my briefcase. She pointed to the large bundle that was placed on the witness stand. But I hadn't seen this before and didn't have a clue where each piece of evidence was if I needed to refer to it. I walked confidently towards the witness stand and I was determined to be articulate when I deliver my evidence. Unfortunately, I had no experience of speaking as a court witness and when I was questioned about things that seemed unrelated to my claim, that threw me off track and I started babbling like an imbecile.

After the general introductions, who I was and where I lived, the police barrister stood up, mispronounced my name and then apologised and continued mispronouncing it throughout his questioning.

"Mr Ma-hone."

"Yes."

"Can I ask you to look at page 65 of the bundle in front of you, the terms and conditions of your employment?"

"Yes?"

"Your hours were 7.30 to 11am and 2.30 to 6pm, do you agree?"

"Yes."

"The basic hours were seven hours a day, thirty-eight and a half hours a week. Agree?"

"Yes."

"It's not part time work is it?"

"It was advertised as a part time job," I replied, "I can bring in the advert that says 'part time driving job'."

"You label it as part time but the contract says thirty-eight and a half hours a week."

"So? What's this got to do with the police evicting me?"

"Remove the label; it's a full time job," insisted Buckett.

"Why don't you ask me about the police removing me from my home?" I said.

The judge interrupted. "Mr Mahon you are not here to ask questions, you're here to answer them."

"Sorry Your Honour," I said but inside I contemplated telling the Judge to instruct Mr Buckett to stick to the facts about my eviction. I also wanted to tell Judge Kay what I thought of his opening opinion and how prejudiced it sounded.

Stay polite I told myself even though I wanted to shout from the rafters that whether the job was full time or part time was inconsequential to my case. I knew I had to tone down my forceful nature and just answer each question clearly and concisely even though I considered the line of questioning stupid. But of course Buckett, was trying to rile me up and it was working. I was getting annoyed at having to answer questions that had nothing to do with the police evicting me. Then the line of questioning changed.

"You claim that PC Hughes said 'I know Liz and she wants you out'."

"Yes. I thought it was a funny thing to say," I replied.

"When your solicitor wrote the letter on your behalf, if you look at page 220 in the bundle, a letter written by RFB Solicitors on 20 December 2004, there is no mention of those crucial words on which you rely: I know Liz and she wants you out."

"Ah yes," I stumbled, unsure how to explain, "the problem I've had with this case and solicitors in general is I tell them what happened and they write what they think is the best way to phrase what happened which is slightly different to what actually happened."

"Mr Ma-hone that comment, I know Liz, in your mind if correct speaks to a form of conspiracy, the police not being even-handed. I know Liz, suggests that the officer knows her personally; there is some kind of history. Do you agree?"

"Well that insinuates that to me," I agreed. "When he said it, I thought, oh this is not official."

"The letter you had your solicitor write on your behalf does not mention this. There is no comment made of this," insisted Buckett.

"I told the solicitor and he didn't write it," I said.

"Right so this is your case, you told your solicitor the comment but he refused to include it in the letter."

"He didn't refuse," I started to explain. "He dictated the letter and sent it off on my behalf."

"And you were happy with the contents of the letter?" asked Buckett.

"I went along with the solicitor because I thought he knew best what to say. All I wanted to do was complain about the action of the officers. That's all I wanted to do. To go into minor details, well that's something I thought would be brought up in court like now."

"You think if the police had simply left that night and had spoken to both of you, do you think there would have been an argument between the two of you?"

"No." I said firmly, "I had to get up at six o'clock so I wanted to go back to sleep."

"Do you think anything would have happened?"

"Well I might have asked her why she called the police. It did frighten me and I would have gone to my solicitor the next day –which I did anyway – and asked him what can I do now? Maybe I should get out of the house in case she lies even more. Like I say, I was frightened because I had never had dealings with the police."

"I didn't suggest you did. If the police had left you there that night, gone away with the two of you in the house, there would have been an argument."

"You don't know that, I don't know that, nobody knows that."

"You wouldn't have stood for what had happened. There would have been an argument."

"You don't know me," I insisted, "I would have just gone to bed. I probably would have asked her why she involved the police but I know what would have happened. She would have turned and walked away and the conversation would have been over."

"And you would have erupted like you did when the two letters were given to you that month."

"I didn't erupt about two letters."

"Yes you did," insisted Bucket. "When the officers arrived you were shouting and swearing."

"If I was shouting and swearing why was I not arrested, not charged, not prosecuted?"

"Mr Mahon I've told you, you are not here to ask questions," insisted the judge.

"Sorry. You weren't there, I was," I now felt really annoyed, "Why does everybody believe Liz and nobody believes me?"

"Mr Ma-hone, we are looking for the reality," said Bucket.

"But it's untrue. What Liz is saying is totally untrue. There is not one word of truth in her statement and if you look at the officer's statements and Liz's statement you'll see they don't match. Someone is lying. Are you saying the police are not lying or are you saying Liz is not lying because they both say different things happened? The police statement matches my account of what happened that night. Liz's statement says there was shouting and swearing, the next door neighbour says there was no shouting and swearing and he saw the police arrive. Only Liz is the one who claims that this happened."

There was a moment of silence and I realised that I might have been a bit forceful with my reply.

I momentarily lost concentration on what was happening. I felt I had just hung myself and I could feel the rope slipping round my neck. All

I needed now was the judge to kick away the chair. Buckett continued bombarding me for two and a half hours with questions about my health, my taxes and my income, all of which I felt was a diversion from the facts.

Judge Kay continuously interrupted with his smart remarks that he didn't believe me, didn't believe my doctor and laughed at the psychiatrist's report which claimed I had suffered post- traumatic stress because of the actions of the police.

"Does anyone know who this doctor Nandy is?" smirked the judge.

Everyone shook their heads, "No".

But Ms Annard stood up and asked Judge Kay if he had been medically trained. That knocked the wind out of him for a moment and he then had to admit he could no longer pass comment on the psychiatric report.

I left the court thinking of all the things I should have said and all the things I shouldn't have said and kicking myself for being so inane. Jenna told me I did well but I felt I had come across as being too forceful and that could be interpreted in a detrimental way. The first day was over and I was completely exhausted.

CHAPTER 20

◇◇◇◇◇

AMNESIA

It was the second day in court and I was called again to be questioned about my tax returns.

I looked out into the court room to see Maurice, Simon and his friend, my son Caolan as well as Jenna and Masako. I was hoping and praying I wouldn't let myself down in front of these friends. Ms Annard said she had never seen so many supporters with a client.

Mr Buckett continued with his obsession about my tax returns, my earnings and if I was just taking the police to court to get money, as he said, "claw back what you think you are entitled to?"

"I'm not doing this for money." I replied, "If I were doing this for money I wouldn't have spent eight years and thousands of pounds trying to prove the police have lied. No amount of money from the police is going to change my life but what they've done and the accusations they made about me has changed my life."

"You felt by bringing an action against the police the damages would enable you to re-open that settlement against Mrs Keenan."

"No!" I snapped and then I hesitated. "I know I can't do that now. All I wanted to do was clear my name."

"The only reason why I'm asking these questions Mr Ma-hone is because if you look at page 34 of the supplement bundle, and if you look at the last paragraph and what you said at the end is illuminating. 'I would hope if these proceedings are successful it may mean that I will be able to re-open the beneficial interest proceedings involving Liz Keenan.' Do you see that?"

I looked at the page and remembered that back then I thought I had to prove the police had lied before I could make my claim against Liz. What I thought was common sense did not match my little knowledge of the law and I never in my wildest dreams imagined it would take so long to try and bring the police to court to clear my name. Buckett was trying to misconstrue my motives and of course I know that's what he's being paid to do.

"You would see that property go up in value of £100,000 and the true motivation of your actions in these proceedings is to try to re-open your claim against Liz Keenan," said Buckett.

"Liz was using the police report to blacken my name and it weakened my claim," I replied. "All I asked for was the £20,000 I had put into the property."

"So is it your case that you would have left the property much earlier in December?"

"Oh yes. I would have been out that door quicker than you can say - ketchup." I immediately replied. "I was advised to stay by my solicitor, in fact by two solicitors."

He went over the same old ground as the day before, accusing me of only staying in the property to get money and no matter what I said he insisted it was about nothing else. I wanted to shout and scream, "Why do you not listen?" I felt I was losing the argument and his questioning was now starting to pierce my confidence. Then he turned his attention to why I hadn't left the property sooner.

"Okay," interrupted Judge Kay, "The police accused you of being aggressive which is really the worst part of their allegations. They accused you of swearing at Ms Keenan; what stopped you, if you wanted to stay in your job, commuting or finding somewhere to live locally, not necessarily in Hemel, Watford, somewhere very close by?"

"I don't want to live in Watford!" I stuttered, not really sure what my answer should be. "I have friends and family in London and I wanted to get away from Hertfordshire police."

I couldn't think of an answer that sounded plausible. I was flustered. Even though I had lots of answers, I just couldn't think of one.

"Within a month you decided that Hertfordshire police had it in for you?" asked Judge Kay.

That's when I mentioned the incident in 2005 of the two uniformed officers pulling me over in my car. My wounds were still raw then and my paranoia told me they were only picking on me because I had made a complaint about Hughes and Thurston. I told the judge what the officers gave as a reason for stopping me: "driving while wearing sunglasses" and I told him what I said to the officer. "I think there are worse crimes on the streets of England than somebody driving around wearing tinted glasses!" and that was the end of my credibility. I may as well have told him I saw a leprechaun singing the blues at Stonehenge.

"Mr Ma-hone, this is pure invention on your part," laughed Mr Buckett, "Why have you never mentioned this before?"

"Forget it then!" I said, "I only mentioned it because Judge Kay wanted to know why I left Hemel and that was one of the reasons."

"Is this mentioned anywhere in the statements?" asked Judge Kay.

"Well, I didn't mention it – I didn't complain because, if the police wouldn't accept my complaint about being evicted, they certainly wouldn't be interested in me being stopped for wearing sunglasses."

"Mr Mahone you haven't in eight years mentioned a traffic stop," said Mr Buckett, "May I suggest you're struggling for a reason to supply why you didn't stay in Hemel to carry on working in your job."

"Well," I mumbled, "strike it out then. You're not going to believe anything I say anyway."

"We will strike it out," agreed Mr Buckett.

I felt so stupid. How could I let myself be dragged down this alleyway to imbecility? Jenna told me later that I shouldn't have told that story because it sounded ridiculous and stupid even though it did happen and as far as Mr Buckett and Judge Kay were concerned it was as believable as seeing flying pigs playing football. Now I know why nobody believes I was woken and kicked out of my home. I left the witness stand a less confident man than I had arrived. When Maurice came up to me afterwards, face as white as a ghost, he warned, "Pete if you don't stay calm you are going to lose this case." I sat there silent among the voices of doom thinking to myself I must have blown any chance of persuading the judge of my innocence.

I half-listened to my son, Caolan's evidence when he was called to the stand because I just couldn't stop thinking about my disastrous performance. But when Caolan announced that, "Dad had changed because of the police action," I started to choke up. The fact that Caolan had witnessed the police refusing to record my complaint didn't seem to interest Judge Kay what-so-ever. Caolan told me later how disappointed he was that Mr Buckett hadn't cross-examined him.

PC Thurston was then called to the stand and that's when I regained full attention. I wanted to hear what this man had to say for himself. I wasn't angry when I saw him, just curious to know what his story was going to be. Ms Annard stood and organised her paperwork for a few seconds then looked up at officer Thurston. He appeared to be shy in his white open neck shirt without a jacket and he also looked anxious, constantly hesitated before giving his answers. Thurston claimed his lack of progress with paperwork and rules of policing were not out of the ordinary and that was why he was partnered with PC Hughes. Hughes had more experience and had been in the police force for about three or four years before leaving in the late 1990's to go travelling. PC Hughes re-joined in 2002 and fate led him and Thurston to my door on that unfortunate night in 2004. "Brilliant" I thought as I slumped back in my chair with my head in my hands. "Two years in the force and Thurston still hadn't a clue what he was doing!"

Mr Buckett objected to certain question thrown at Thurston but Ms Annard seemed very relaxed and unmoved by Buckett's constant interruptions. Thurston had been interviewed by Professional Standards back in 2006 when there was an investigation into the incident. He had denied all knowledge of what had happened on that evening. So I sat there with fixed attention while Ms Annard fired her questions. I wanted to hear his excuses.

"In your interview you are asked if you knew of any previous actions that were taken regarding the allegations. And you responded: 'No I don't know any background to the job at all.' Did you have no previous knowledge of Mr Mahon or any issues arising from the property or Ms Keenan?"

"Erm..." Thurston stood thinking and there was a long gap. It seemed to last for ages. It was a gap long enough to write a book on 'How to answer awkward questions'. Then he spoke. "I wasn't aware of any background of the job."

"Can I ask you to turn to page 71 of the bundle in front of you? This is a printout of the crime report and it suggests that Ms Keenan came into Hemel Hempstead Police Station on 14 December and if you can see that the entry appears to be made on the 20 December at eight minutes past six in the morning?"

"Yes. That's correct," said Thurston.

"So although the entry is saying that she came into the police station on the 14 December, it has not been put into the computer until 20 December?"

"Yes."

"And if you look at page 77, this is a similar police printout and the date is 14 December again. And then at the bottom it says 'Officer' and it has your name and your number."

"Yes. That's correct," agreed Thurston.

"And is it correct that you were the officer who was on the front desk when she came in on the 14 December?"

"No. That's not correct."

"Can you explain how your name is on this document?"

"Yes. This log came in on the 14 December. It was closed and then reopened on the 20 December. The controller would have picked one of the officers that were in the vehicle and closed it under their name."

That didn't make any sense to me; but nothing about the police and this matter had ever made sense. So Thurston was confirming that anyone could write a crime report even if they were not present at the incident.

I was wondering what Judge Kay was making of Thurston's answer and I also realised I should have gone to the toilet before we entered the court room.

"Were you told that Elizabeth Keenan had rung the police station at 10.30 that evening?" continued Ms Annard.

"I can't recall being aware of that. No."

"Were you aware that PC Hughes had telephoned her back to check that Mr Mahon was in the property just before you left?"

"No. I wasn't aware of that," said Thurston.

"And when you arrived was Mr Mahon sleeping in the living room on the ground floor?"

"Erm..." Once again Thurston stood thinking.

"By which I mean it was clear that there was a makeshift bed there?" continued Ms Annard.

Thurston stood silent for a few more seconds then he spoke. "I can't recall the exact layout," Thurston mumbled, "I can't say as to what he was sleeping on."

"But there was a makeshift bed that you could see?" asked Ms Annard.

"I can't remember that," he replied.

"But in your statement you say 'he had just woken up and he wasn't happy that he had to go' is that correct?" she asked.

Buckett then jumped up. "Can I just – sorry to interrupt. What he actually said that I noted on the tape was 'As far as I'm aware, he'd just woken up.'"

"So you are disputing that?" the judge asked Buckett.

"That is what I believe it says," replied Mr Buckett.

Ms Annard offered to stop the hearing to sit down and work out if the transcript matched the tape recording. But Judge Kay frowned at Ms Annard's suggestion that Mr Buckett had made a mistake. She tried to explain to the judge that the transcript was supplied by my solicitor, Lawrence, but because she had not received it until Monday, the morning of the hearing, did not have the opportunity to sit down and go through it to make sure it was word perfect. Meanwhile I couldn't concentrate on what was happening, I needed to go to the toilet. Should I slip out in the hope that no one would notice or should I raise my hand to be excused? I sat with my legs crossed wondering what was the court etiquette on toilet use?

"Let us just go ahead and see what happens," said Judge Kay, looking slightly bored.

"PC Thurston, is it your evidence that Mr Mahon had just woken up or not?" asked Ms Annard.

"I can't recall whether he had just woken up or not," replied Thurston.

"Do you have any reason to doubt what you said in your interview in February 2006?"

"No. I don't."

"It is correct, is it not, that Mr Mahon was in his dressing gown?" asked Ms Annard.

And Thurston paused again. "I can't recall that," he mumbled.

"You do not recall going upstairs with Mr Mahon and watching him put on some clothes?"

"I don't recall that either, no."

"And is it not, that when Ms Keenan opened the front door to you she then turned and opened the door to the living room and turned on the lights and said: 'Peter, Peter, the police want to have a word with you'?"

"Again, I can't recall that," said Thurston.

"Is it correct, that Mr Mahon then got up and put on his dressing gown?"

"I can't recall that."

Simon lent forward and whispered into my ear, "Tell her to ask him, what the fuck does he remember?"

I was now more concerned about my bladder. I needed to go – immediately.

"And Ms Keenan then spoke to PC Hughes separately and you stood in the doorway of the living room with Mr Mahon?" continued Ms Annard.

"PC Hughes did speak to the female and I waited with the male."

"And in your statement you said, 'When PC Hughes came back from speaking to the female, I was basically waiting outside the door where the gentleman was sleeping or where his bed is'. And PC Hughes said to you, 'he has to leave.' Is that correct?"

"Yes. That's correct." agreed Thurston.

"It is correct, is it not, that after PC Hughes indicated this to you, you then asked Mr Mahon to leave?"

"Sorry, can you repeat the question?" stuttered Thurston.

"Yes," said Ms Annard. "After PC Hughes said to you: 'he has to leave' you then asked Mr Mahon to leave?"

Thurston hesitated again for a moment. He stood thinking. "Yes, he would have been asked to leave after that." he said.

"Just to be clear, PC Hughes had not spoken to Mr Mahon prior to this?"

"No. I don't recall him talking to him prior to that."

"And Hughes only spoke to the female for a minute?"

"I wouldn't be able to recall the exact amount of time that he spoke to her," he stuttered.

"And you had not had an opportunity to speak to the female until after the male had left the house?" asked Ms Annard.

"Yes. That's correct."

"And after Mr Mahon left the house, you and PC Hughes had a cup of tea with Ms Keenan?"

"Yes. That's correct."

"Huh!" screamed Jenna out loud from the back of the room.

"I do not know what is so funny," interrupted Judge Kay, "That answer seems to have amused some people at the back of the court."

"I do not think it was so much amusement as surprise, Your Honour," said Ms Annard.

"Perhaps if they could refrain from reacting," insisted Judge Kay.

I looked at Jenna and she smiled at me. I smiled back. But I couldn't stand it anymore. I was bursting to go to the toilet. I leaned forward and spoke to my barrister. She didn't quite hear me so I raised my voice. "I really need to go to the toilet!"

"Your Honour, could we have a very short break? Mr Mahon rather urgently needs to go to the bathroom," asked Ms Annard.

"Yes certainly, yes, of course," said the judge. "Do not speak to anybody about your evidence."

I wasn't sure who Judge Kay was talking to but I didn't care because I had no intention of making conversation on my way to the toilet. I had to get out of that room before I flooded the floor and having that pee was the most pleasurable experience in this excruciating two-day court drama.

When the court resumed, Thurston continued to live in the land of amnesia but one of the few things he did remember was PC Hughes had written the crime report that had accused me of shouting and swearing.

"PC Thurston, you have made reference in your statement to this being a domestic violence incident," continued Ms Annard; "It is correct, is it not, that Ms Keenan had never reported to the police that Mr Mahon had been physically violent to her?"

"No. She had not, not that I know of," replied Thurston.

"And if you turn to page 72 in the bundle in front of you, it says there: 'Female has called the police on the 20 December stating male has returned to the address. Police arrived and male became verbally aggressive and swearing and he was asked to leave by the police.' So from the evidence that you have given today, you would say that that is not an accurate description of what happened?"

"When we arrived I don't recall him becoming verbally aggressive or swearing, no," agreed Thurston.

"I have no further questions... Your Honour, actually, could I just check?" And she turned to me. I told her to ask him about the 'Management action' he had received from a senior officer. This is apparently a disciplinary measure given to a police officer explaining how his actions did not meet the required standard expected to carry out his duties. She turned to Thurston.

"I understand a more senior police officer had words of advice with you about this incident and when you were asked in the interview if you would have done anything differently you said no?"

"Yes. That's correct," said Thurston.

"And following the words of advice that you have had from a senior officer now, would you change your view?"

Thurston stood thinking and this time it seemed he was not going to answer. Everyone in the court stared at him, hanging on his every breath but he said nothing. I thought he was refusing to speak. It felt as if a life time of silence had past and I was expecting Judge Kay to say something when suddenly Thurston started to talk.

"Of this incident, it's difficult to say how I would deal with it again. I am more experienced now". He stumbled for words. "The way that I would deal with it would be different, would… maybe different because of my experience, so it would be difficult to say how I would deal with it now."

"What the hell did that mean?" I sat there bewildered at his answer. I was half expecting the judge to ask for clarification but nothing was said. Maurice came up to me afterwards and said he noticed the judge's face was starting to change. I hadn't noticed because my attention had been focused entirely on Thurston but that made me smile for the first time in two days. Surely Judge Kay's initial impressions were changing now.

CHAPTER 21

◇◇◇◇◇

IS THERE A PART 36?

It was my last trip to Luton and I was exhausted. What I had experienced in the County Court had not lived up to what I had expected. It was very unsatisfactory. I was drained of enthusiasm and fed-up with all the contention I experience just to be believed. I told my barrister that I had decided to wear a black tie, just in case I lost. She looked puzzled then looked at my tie and smiled when she got the joke. She asked if I would be satisfied with just getting my costs back and I told her, "it was all I had ever expected" and she said "good". I had gone into this battle with a determination to find justice and a passion to expose corruption. I've come out disillusioned about exposing corruption but still passionate about finding justice.

We all piled into the courtroom and took our usual places. Judge Kay walked into the court looking a bit more serious than he had done for the past two days. He announced he was not going to give a written summing up but instead would verbally sum up his decision today. I wondered why. And when I tried to get a transcript of his judgement weeks later, I was informed that two of the microphones had been switched off for the entire three-day hearing. The only court microphone working was my barrister's. My paranoia immediately clicked in and assumed it was a conspiracy but I also had a bit of luck on my side, for unbeknown to me Jenna had recorded some of the hearing on her iPod. Mr Buckett summed up the case for the police by rambling on with technical legal points until everybody was yawning except Simon who had fallen asleep. I thought the barrister was just wasting time or trying to bore Judge Kay into submission so as the police would gain a victory. Ms Annard quickly summed up my case and then Judge Kay said he would deliver his verdict after lunch.

It was a sunny day so I sat with my group of supporters in the sunlight eating sandwiches in the nearby outdoor market cafe close to the courthouse.

When we returned that afternoon Judge Kay immediately began to tell us how he had deliberated on the sources of evidence yet reminding us, it was with his strong opinion that "the Police officers acted with the honest intention of averting any possible confrontation." That's when I thought "why did I bother?" He had made his mind up from the beginning and I hadn't a chance of winning. I found it a struggle to listen to some of the points he felt were obvious while I knew they were not factual.

"...with regards to PC Hughes," Judge Kay continued, "he left the police force in 2005. There is no statement from him. His account of what occurred that night, found in a domestic violence investigation form that said the female was in a distressed state and afraid to be alone in the premises with the male who was refusing to vacate the premises to avoid breach of the peace. Those are sources of evidence I have, to what occurred. I am saying that I don't accept that anybody can recall precise events of what happened that night so I reconstructed the matter the best I can on the balance of probabilities."

He recited his interpretation of what had happened over the past eight years and I lost interest half way through because it all sounded familiar and one sided. I looked out the window and stared at the sky that was now becoming overcast and wondered why there were no birds flying past. Behind me Maurice was nudging Simon to try and keep him awake. Three hours we listened to Judge Kay and it felt longer than the London Marathon. He still felt that the officers had acted in good faith. He must have been asleep during the hearing and I only wished Maurice had been nudging the judge instead of Simon. When he finally finished I was unsure what he had decided. He mumbled something that I thought sounded a bit like 'an award of eighteen per cent costs' and then turned to the police barrister, Mr Buckett and asked him:

"Is there a Part 36?"

Buckett stood up and replied, "No Your Honour, there is no Part 36."

"What!" said Judge Kay, looking surprised? "No Part 36? Then it looks like he's won."

Why was the judge surprised I had won? He seemed more surprised than I did yet it is he who is making the decision. I turned round to Jenna who was all smiles and I said, "What's happening?"

"You've won Dad."

"I have?" I asked, "But didn't the judge only award me eighteen per cent?"

"Not eighteen Dad! Eighty."

"Oh, I thought he said eighteen."

"I think you're going deaf," she laughed.

Maybe it was because I wasn't listening properly to what Judge Kay was saying but it appeared everyone was now congratulating me while I stood shocked. I wanted to win and I fought hard to win but I was still taken aback with the verdict. Not many people beat the police. Masako and Simon continued to voice their opinion that I should have been awarded more but Jenna told them to shut up because the important thing was that I had won and that was all that mattered.

"You don't look very happy Mr Mahon," said Ms Annard.

"I was... I didn't expect the judge to..." I stuttered, unable to get the words out, "he was not on my side."

"Well, you've won," she said, "well done."

"Thank you and well done to you."

"It had a lot to do with the police incompetence," she replied.

I had been told about a 'Part 36 Offer' by my solicitor, Tim King back in 2007 when he explained how it was intended to put pressure on me to accept a settlement out of court. I stubbornly refused to listen to his warning of course. But Tim King was emphasising that there are consequences in relation to costs arising from this. If I reject the Part 36 offer from the police and the judge awards me a lesser amount, then I would be responsible for the other party's costs and my compensation would be swallowed up by the other party's legal costs. I could win but not receive a penny. No wonder Judge Kay was surprised that the police had not made a Part 36 offer. I was convinced Judge Kay had deliberately reduced the amount awarded to me to make sure it would be less than an out of court settlement that he perceived would have come from the police.

I had won my claim on assault, intimidation and breach of my Human Rights with a small award of money for post-traumatic stress disorder. The final amount was over £30,000.

We went outside and suddenly I realised it was over. I had won. What an amazing feat. I had sued the police and won. I needed confirmation to snap me out of the shock I was in after the years of struggling and if it hadn't had been for Jenna continuously shouting, "You've won Dad, you've won!" I don't think it would have sunk in properly. I had proven that Hughes lied, that Liz and her brother Palfrey lied and the whole legal system lied to try and protect the liars.

The journey home was over in a flash because all I could think about was my success. I had achieved something that, deep down inside, I never really thought would come to fruition.

CHAPTER 22

◇◇◇◇◇

ANOTHER MEETING

MIKE PENNING MP
Member of Parliament for Hemel Hempstead
Constituency Office
Hamilton House, 111 Marlowes, Hemel Hempstead, Herts HP1 1BB
Telephone : 01442 450444

Our ref: Mahon-Police 1708.doc

Mr Jeremy Alford
Chief Supt
Hertfordshire Constabulary
Watford Police Station
Shady Lane
Watford
Herts WD17 1DD

17th August 2009

Dear Chief Supt

Mr Peter Mahon

I am writing on behalf of Mr Mahon, whose case I understand is known to you, and who would really appreciate a meeting with you to discuss the issues.

He did take his complaint to the IPCC and both this organisation and the Hertfordshire Constabulary confirm that the Police Officers concerned were in the wrong and Mr Mahon has been compensation.

I do appreciate that, as this case regarding the officers is still outstanding, it might not be appropriate to have a meeting at this point in time. However, once the case has been concluded, I would be grateful if you would be able to meet with me and Mr Mahon to look at the evidence he can present.

This has been a very traumatic case for Mr Mahon and I support his wishes to discuss the situation and other aspects of this case with you in an attempt to prevent this type of situation occurring again.

I look forward to hearing from you.

Yours sincerely,

Mike Penning

8.   'MP's unconditional support.'

HERTFORDSHIRE CONSTABULARY

0 4 SEP 2009

☎ **Direct Line:** 01923 472081
✉ **E-Mail:** jeremy.alford@herts.pnn.police.uk

Ref: JA/KD/07-061/05

1ˢᵗ September 2009

PRIVATE AND CONFIDENTIAL
Mike Penning, MP
Hamilton House
111 Marlowes
Hemel Hempstead
Hertfordshire
HP1 1BB

Dear Mike

Thank you for your letter dated the 17ᵗʰ August 2009 in relation to your client Mr Mahon and your desire for me to meet with him and yourself in an attempt to prevent this type of situation occurring again.

I appreciate that a meeting with Mr Mahon may appear to be a reasonably easy solution to Mr Mahon's issues, however I am sure you will appreciate that this matter has been the subject of considerable proceedings and correspondence between himself and his legal representatives and Hertfordshire Constabulary Legal Services Department and Professional Standards Department. I will seek further advice from our Legal Services Department about such a meeting but I am aware that they are still in active correspondence with Mr Mahon and his legal representatives in relation to this matter and I feel sure that they will advise me that such a meeting at this stage is not appropriate. When I hear back from them I will get back to you.

Please be assured that when it is right and proper to do so and when all outstanding Police complaints and other civil matters are completed I anticipate that such a meeting will be the proper way to draw a line under this affair.

Yours sincerely

Chief Supt Jeremy Alford
Area Commander
Western Area

WESTERN AREA
Watford Police Station, Shady Lane, Watford, Herts, WD17 1DD
Tel: 01923 472000   Fax: 01923 472039

Working together for a safer Hertfordshire

www.herts.police.uk

9.   'Police continue to avoid meeting.'

I started writing to various authorities informing them of my victory and of course I wrote to the Hemel Hempstead MP Mike Penning who had helped me unconditionally for the eight long years. I asked him to help me arrange a meeting with the Chief Superintendent of Hertfordshire to find out if the police would now be prepared to prosecute Liz or ex-PC Hughes or even PC Thurston. It took a further six months to persuade the police to meet with me and at the last minute Chief Superintendent Ball backed out of the meeting and sent a Superintendent Nicholls as his replacement. I wasn't surprised: two other Chief Superintendents had refused to meet with me in the past. The preliminary meeting was to be at the Hemel Hempstead police station and I decided to bring my tape recorder in case something was said that might be denied at a later date. I put forward my request for an investigation into why there had been a crime report falsely stating I was shouting and swearing at the police officers. Superintendent Nicholls assured me he would look into it but it wasn't until two months later that Nicholls requested a meeting with just Mike Penning and not with me. But Mr Penning insisted that I should be present at the meeting.

I arrived early at Hemel police station on that unusually cold day in March 2013 and stood outside the front door because the station was closed. Financial cuts to police funds were causing police stations to have restricted opening hours. Mike Penning, who was Northern Ireland Secretary at the time, had flown from Belfast the previous night so as not to miss the meeting and we stood outside the station waiting for it to open, talking about my home town Belfast and the turmoil it had gone through. Over the years I had requested numerous meetings with the police authorities to find answers to my questions because I considered talking to be more productive. Shouting and protesting would be a waste of time.

We were let in after about half an hour and led upstairs to a small office. After Mr Penning and Superintendent Nicholls finished discussing their passion about motor bikes, Superintendent Nicholls started explaining how he had investigated my request and assured me that the police had taken the matter very seriously. He admitted that Hughes was the officer who had written the crime report and from what he had seen agreed that Hughes had falsified the report. He apologised to me on behalf of the police authority and handed me a copy of the crime report with a correction to Hughes's entry that said: '*Following a recent civil court case it has been established that the male party was not aggressive towards police officers and did not swear at them.*' I accepted his apology but I continued to push the point that someone should be prosecuted. I also felt it should be Hughes, PC Thurston and Mrs Alison Grundy who should apologise to me but I knew that would never happen.

"It has taken you one month to find out that the crime report is false yet the police continued for eight years to accuse me of shouting at the officers," I said. "Would you consider that to be incompetence or a cover-up?"

"Erm…" he hesitated, "I don't consider it a cover up, probably a mistake."

"Eight years is not a mistake," I said.

"I can see why you've lost confidence in Hertfordshire police and why you would think there was some kind of conspiracy, but you must remember that Officer Hughes had just come off a night duty and his bio rhythms were probably all over the place when he wrote the report. PC Hughes is no longer in the organisation, I don't know where he is or what he's doing but I can only apologise and say it has been unfortunate you had to go through this," he continued, "But I must say that Hertfordshire Constabulary is one of the best performing in the country. To prosecute we would have to identify some kind of criminal intent instead of just a mistake..."

"...a mistake?" I interrupted. "This was not a mistake, it was a deliberate smear."

"I'm sorry but we would have to justify using public money to..."

"You can't say that now after wasting public money for eight years victimizing and lying about me."

The superintendent tried to explain that they had changed their computer system and that information about PC Hughes had not been transferred because he was no longer in the force. Even though the superintendent was prepared to admit that Hughes had written a false report he was still trying to excuse the officer for his actions and justify why there would be no prosecutions. Mike Penning said afterwards that Nicholls had probably said more than he was prepared or willing to say but he didn't think the police were interested in taking it any further.

"Even if they did think they should prosecute ex-PC Hughes, the Crown Prosecution Service would not consider it. They have this ambiguous wording, 'is it in the public interest?' and I would argue that it is for the integrity of the police and in the interest of the police to prosecute," said Mr Penning, "but of course they know full well that it won't go any further."

I walked away wondering if this was the end of my battle or the end of my war. I was surprised how long the fight had lasted but I still was prepared to fight a little longer.

I continued writing letters to the police authorities for another year or so. The tension and stress I had been under for over eight years was slowly starting to evaporate and I was beginning to feel relaxed again. I had been a fighter who had fought a long bloody battle with a powerful opponent and I was very tired, badly bruised and I needed a rest. Even though I felt I had achieved what a lot of people said I hadn't a hope in hell in getting near to, I also felt it was a hollow victory with no prosecutions.

I rested for a while and then decided I would try once more to unravel the lying arm of the law. I started with another letter to Chief Constable Andy Bliss requesting a meeting even though he had refused three times to meet with me.

◇◇◇◇◇

CHAPTER 23

IS IT IN THE PUBLIC INTEREST?

I was very stupid and naive to have believed that the one place to find truth and honesty was in the hands of the police. I expected them to sort the matter out sooner than later and I thought it was going to be resolved within a couple of days or even a week but the police in their wisdom, incompetence or corruption turned a minor civil matter into a major, unbelievable, criminal cock-up. But of course they deny that. It's a shame that a few rotten coppers have stained the reputation of the hard working honest policeman. I know the accusations made by ex-PC Hughes and my ex-partner, Liz, could have been a lot worse and even though I never found hard evidence that they colluded, there is too much circumstantial evidence for it to be brushed aside entirely. Of course there is also the possibility that Hughes may have been stupid enough to have believed Liz. But I think there was more to it than that because Hughes had been seen calling at Liz's house for a number of weeks after the incident.

This little brush with the law has turned me into a compulsive com- plainer and an obsessive letter writer whereas before I wouldn't have bothered. Purely out of frustration, I made a complaint to Luton Coun- ty Court about the extra expense I incurred when I tried to get a tran- script of my hearing from an inaudible court recording. No explanation was given why two of the court microphones had been switched off during the whole three-day hearing. Surely the whole legal system is not trying to stop me receiving justice. Of course not, I'm just being para- noid. I wrote to the court with my bill of extra costs and even though they admitted they had made the mistake, they still refused to pay. So I informed them I would be taking court proceedings. Normally I would have accepted their excuse and given up but not now. I was only claiming £121.00 and I was doing it as a point of principal. I was offered £69.00 so I told them where to stick it. I wrote a pre-action letter stating I would be taking Luton County Court to the small claims court. I didn't know if anyone had ever taken a court to court but I wasn't frightened to try, just to prove a point. They backed down one month later and paid the full amount.

I continued writing letters to people I was told oversee the running of an efficient and effective police force like the Commissioner of Police and Crime, the Home Secretary and even the Prime Minister. My experience of the Police and Crime Commissioner of Hertfordshire was to say at the least, disappointing, when he did not respond to my two letters. On my third attempt his assistant sent me a reply. The assistant's letter repeated every allegation the police had made against me and said it was 'not in the public interest' to prosecute anyone. I replied pointing out it was not his opinion I had requested, it was the Commissioner's opinion I wanted and I demanded an apology from him for regurgitating false accusations that had been proven and admitted by the police as untrue. I was so angry I told him I considered his job as, "not in the public interest and a waste of public money". That comment was probably the real reason why he didn't apologise.

My letter to the Home Secretary at the Home Office ended up being re-diverted to a Mrs Solomon in Cornwall.

I know it sounds like something I've made up and I'm sure by now you're thinking my story is a tall Irish yarn but a Mrs Solomon did write to me explaining that she had written to Dominic Grieve MP, asking for his help regarding negligent solicitors in her area. She received my letter as a reply. By this time, I had not received a reply or any correspondence from the Home Secretary so I decided to write again, only this time I deliberately wrote a sarcastic letter because I felt I had nothing more to lose.

"Dear Home Secretary, considering I haven't received a reply from you I assume you gave it to Dominic Grieve MP who in turn has sent it to Mrs Solomon for her comments and opinions. I am not familiar with the seating arrangements at the Home Office but maybe you and Mr Grieve's are sharing a desk. It's nice to see the government are making cutbacks. If it would be possible to reply to my letter with some kind of explanation or alternatively send it to Mrs Solomon in Cornwall, then she could reply to me with an explanation."

The Home Secretary's reply was short and unambiguous: *"the Home Office will only consider any new points that you wish to make."* There was no apology for the mix-up.

Still I continued to write to anyone I thought might listen and the reply from 10 Downing Street was just as infuriating as every other government department letter I had received.

"Dear Mr Mahon, thank you for contacting Mr Cameron who appreciates you taking the time and trouble to get in touch. I hope you will appreciate that as the Home Office is best placed to respond to the matter you raise, I am forwarding your letter to them so that they may reply to you directly."

But they never replied and it wouldn't have surprised me if that letter had evaporated into space on a mission to Mars or sent to Mrs Solomon in Cornwall.

I am still not sure whether the system is designed to malfunction or whether the people are designed to malpractice and so with that thought in my head and with the help of Mike Penning MP, I wrote to the Home Affairs Select Committee asking for a public enquiry into corruption and misfeasance within Hertfordshire Constabulary. Mr Keith Vaz MP, Chairman of the Home Affairs Committee, replied telling me that he had written to Dame Anne Owers, Chair of the IPCC asking her to address the issues raised by me. But my experience of the IPCC didn't give me confidence that anything would happen. I did receive a letter that had been forwarded to Mr Penning MP saying they were dealing with my complaint and the writer claimed she was the IPCC's Commissioner with responsibility for Hertfordshire Police. She explained that the IPCC had given dispensation to Hertfordshire Constabulary not to investigate my complaint against Alison Grundy, (the Legal Services solicitor who had spent eight years defending the officers). I found this excuse so painful to read that I threw the letter into the bin. I replied to Dame Owers and the IPCC Commissioner enclosing a copy of the letter I had received in 2010 from the IPCC that clearly stated that no dispensation had been granted. I pointed out that Hertfordshire Police had lied to them as they had lied about me but that piece of information was also ignored. Months later I received another reply from the IPCC and this time they agreed that no dispensation had been given but informed me that a thorough investigation had been completed and no further investigating would be done.

The matter was now closed. I stood scratching my head. I may be ignorant of the law but I'm smart enough to realise how stupid I would be to accept that excuse. Considering all evidence hadn't been looked at how on earth was a thorough investigation done?

I didn't receive the money I was awarded for another year. I didn't bother to chase for payment because money was not the real reason I took Hertfordshire Constabulary to court. I left all the legal stuff with the costs draftsman who had helped me with my claim against the IPCC in 2007. She told me to leave it with her and she would deal with all the formalities. Six months passed and still my bill of costs from her did not arrive. I phoned and emailed but all I got was excuses and promises that the bill would be ready soon. It didn't really bother me too much but friends kept asking, "When will you get your money?" I thought, maybe I should take a stronger interest and insist on a release date. So I tried phoning the costs draftsman again but this time nobody was answering. I tried emailing but nobody was replying. I was starting to wonder why it was taking so long for my bill of costs to be complied. I phoned the company that the costs draftsman worked for and left desperate messages of urgency because I didn't have a bill of costs to present to the police. Then one day out of the blue my mobile rang and it was the costs draftsman. She apologised and said she was having difficulties with family issues and personal illness.

"But it's almost a year now," I said, "Why is it taking so long?"

"I've been away and I've also been ill," she replied. But that sounded like an excuse that she really couldn't be bothered.

"Are you working for the police?" I asked.

That's when she hesitated before admitting she had been diagnosed with cancer and was in and out of hospital receiving chemotherapy. I was just about to give her a telling off and thank God I hadn't. I was so relieved I had kept my mouth shut. All I could do was apologise and offer her my sympathy. I was now in the awkward position of whether I forget about my money or employ another costs draftsman to compile a new bill of costs. Speaking to my solicitor, Lawrence, I discovered that the process for the costs claim should have started within three months after my case had concluded. We had taken too long to complete the bill of costs and this meant I wouldn't get interest on the amount awarded by the court. Lawrence contacted the new legal firm of top lawyers in Manchester that Hertfordshire Constabulary were now employing. The police were prepared to spend even more public money trying to stop me receiving my awarded money. The Manchester firm threatened court proceedings which, as they said, would result in me receiving nothing. I would have to go to court again to fight for my awarded money and this hearing would cost me approximately £4000. Even though they were threatening that I would receive nothing, the Manchester lawyers did make me an offer to settle out of court so I took from that I still had a chance of receiving something.

"I will not take a penny less than the full amount of my costs," I said to Lawrence and he started laughing.

"If I have to go to court then I will go to court." I declared.

He warned me that I might get less than I expected and I would have the extra cost of going to court and the cost of employing a new costs draftsman as well as the cost of a barrister. There were so many costs I could end up spending the awarded amount of money trying to receive the awarded amount of money.

"I don't care," I replied.

A couple of weeks past and I started reconsidering if I really wanted to continue with more court battles especially over money. It was considered my fault that I didn't submit my bill of costs on time and the police were taking advantage of the time delay to try and refuse paying me anything. I decided not to discuss it with any of my supporters because I knew it was a decision I had to make myself without other people's influence. I eventually decided, with Lawrence's advice, to make a counter-offer and if that was rejected I could still accept their original offer. But they did increase their offer and with a little bit more bargaining I got what I wanted. I was awarded a few pounds short of £30,000.

I flew back to Northern Ireland to pay my cousin Clare the money she had lent me six years previous and to thank my friend Gerry Tweedie for his encouragement and support. I re-started my life and regained the confidence to pursue again the things that I loved doing; music and film-making. It took me longer than I thought to feel any relief from the trauma I had experience but even now friends and colleagues still continue to ask, "is this the last chapter?" When a friend asked me if I regretted taking on the police I just shrugged my shoulders and told him, "The more we're willing to risk the more alive we are. You can put that on my gravestone!" I laughed.

As for ex-PC Hughes, he sold his house in Luton and disappeared. And for Liz, I wasn't surprised when a friend told me he accidentally discovered her on a free internet dating site, stating she was, '*looking for a man.*' She sold the house she had fought hard to keep in Hemel Hempstead and moved to Milton Keynes in 2014.

Friends and family couldn't understand why I continued to write to the Chief Constable of Hertfordshire asking for a meeting. I wrote and wrote but with no success. Eventually, maybe because of my complaint to the Home Affairs Select Committee, I received a reply from the police. Two years had passed; with my energy finally spent and my enthusiasm waning, the police had now offered me a meeting on 6 August 2014. I went through all the paperwork I had accumulated from my eight-year fight and bundled together letters and statements I intended to present as the reason why I felt there should be prosecutions. I rushed things, didn't fully pay attention to detail and foolishly thought I could present most of my evidence from memory. After all, I had been writing statements about the same old argument for a very long time so I should know the facts off by heart. I was told the meeting would be with the Deputy Chief Constable but then again I wasn't sure. I had received so many letters from so many different job titles, Superintendents, Chief Superintendents, Assistant Chief Superintendents, Detective Superintendents and of course Commander Chief Superintendents and that's not including Inspectors and all the Assistants and Deputies.

The police are very top heavy. For all I knew I could end-up having a meeting with the Deputy Assistant Chief Superintendent of Maintenance Inspectors and Supervisors.

Maurice agreed to have a dress rehearsal with me to see if he noticed any weaknesses in my argument. I sat in his living room quoting excerpts from my bundle of papers stumbling, hesitating and then fumbling through the points that I felt were being ignored.

"Stop!" he shouted, "You're starting to annoy me and you will certainly annoy them. You're not going to get anywhere unless you prepare. You will look stupid trying to find bits of paper and they will lose interest. You've worked hard to get this meeting so don't blow it. You must prepare an agenda."

So with two days to go before the meeting I panicked, rushed home and sat in front of my computer trying to write a proper agenda.

◇◇◇◇◇

CHAPTER 24

THE LYING ARM OF THE LAW

My now constant companion Simon agreed to come with me to Hatfield Police Station to meet with Hertfordshire police. We arrived early but couldn't find any spaces in the police car park so we drove around until we saw a spot outside an Indian restaurant. Simon's eyes lit up.

"Maybe we could eat there later", he grunted.

I walked into the police station full of anticipation that this meeting would be seminal to something final. The girl on reception told us to wait until someone could see us and a few minutes later we were approached by a woman I mistakenly took as one of the people we were due to meet. I started formal introductions but she was just the secretary sent to take us upstairs to where the meeting would be held. I felt like a right plonker! We followed the secretary into a large room where we were introduced to Assistant Chief Constable Ball and a female Detective Chief Superintendent Swinburne. We all sat around a large oval table and I opened my briefcase, took out my paper work and switched on my tape recorder. Swinburne also placed her tape machine on the table. Ball was dressed in his police uniform and Swinburne was dressed casually in a skirt, jacket and blouse.

The opening few minutes didn't go as planned. I started feeling nervous because Swinburne continuously told me to be quiet when I tried to speak. She was dominating the meeting while I was stuttering out incomplete sentences that were being ignored. This was not the way I expected things to go and my carefully prepared agenda was just being brushed aside. Why was I suddenly feeling nervous? I had no reason to be nervous but yet I was. I felt the meeting was coming to an end before it had even begun. My hands started shaking, my thoughts became jumbled and I couldn't get a foothold into the debate. But Simon calmly asked the necessary questions while forcefully reminding both Ball and Swinburne where the police had gone wrong. I was glad he was there. As the meeting progressed, I tried to explain why I had requested the meeting, emphasising that there should be prosecutions but they didn't seem that interested. I wanted them to tell me why it had taken so long for the police to admit that I hadn't sworn at the two officers.

"I'm happy to deal with that," said Swinburne. "Mr Mahon, PC Hughes and PC Thurston have never said you swore at them."

"What!" I stopped because it just took my breath away. Did I hear right? I didn't expect this.

"I'll tell you where that came from," she said.

This was a shockwave out of the blue. I had listened for years to the police solicitor, Alison Grundy, claiming that the officers witnessed me 'shouting and swearing' and now I was about to hear another version from these two people who appeared to be part of this ever increasing extension of the lying arm of the law.

"Actually Detective Inspector Fantom reviewed the complaint after your Judicial Review in 2007 and in his report he basically says in his summary about Mr Mahon swearing at the officers. He then later says '*I seem to have made an error and that wasn't the case*'.

If I could direct you to what the officers had said. PC Hughes says, *'Police arrive and male became verbally aggressive and swearing and he was asked to leave by police'*. That does not say he was aggressive and swearing at them."

"So who was I aggressive and swearing at?" I asked.

"He says generally," claimed Swinburne. "Mr Mahon, to be fair, they never said that in the first place."

After ten long, stressful and sometimes frustrating years of being accused of swearing at the two officers, these senior officers have suddenly decided to do a complete about turn. I reminded them that Allison Grundy had continuously maintained I had sworn at the officers.

"That's because she relied on Detective Inspector Fantom's report," claimed Swinburne.

"No! no! no!" I insisted, "The letter that Allison Grundy wrote making those accusations was written on 1 July 2005. Fantom's report was not written until 2007."

"Inspector Fantom sits in on your initial meeting with Allison Grundy?" interrupted Ball.

Simon then spoke and suddenly the conversation went off on a different direction about who wrote the correction in the crime report and who had I been verbally aggressive at. I had to try to bring it back to the point that I was trying to make about Allison Grundy claiming I was verbally aggressive towards the officers.

"That was based on the information from Fantom's report," said Ball.

It didn't seem to register with these senior officers that the police solicitor, Allison Grundy, had accused me of swearing before Fantom's report was even written and Grundy continued to accuse me of swearing at the officers long after Fantom's report was released.

"Just for the benefit of the tape," stated Ball, "it's very important we clear up what the report actually says. The most pertinent point to this debate is *'Liz Keenan has called police on 20 December stating male has returned to the address. Police arrive and male became verbally aggressive and swearing and he was asked to leave'*."

"So you're saying that's what Liz said?" I asked.

"I'm not saying that at all," replied Ball, "Liz Keenan was there and we've read her statement and I think that also clarifies the matter."

"Clarifies the matter?" I said, "I think it confuses the matter."

I wasn't sure if these were clever tactics by the two officers trying to cloud the issues or whether I was not quite grasping their explanation.

"Do you think she's telling the truth?" I asked.

"Well, she's written a statement." said Ball.

"But is she telling the truth?" I said again.

"I've never met Liz Keenan I couldn't say whether she is or…"

"But also the judge said we could rely on that," interrupted Swinburne, "and you accepted the judge's findings."

"No, what the judge said was that the police have to use some common sense to remove someone from the property," said Simon, "if there had have been a subsequent flare-up and she had been attacked."

I looked at Simon and thought; I'm trying to convince them that Liz was lying. Let's forget what the judge said. The conversation was now going round in circles and spinning out of control. I was insisting that PC Hughes had written an accusation of my behaviour that was false and they were trying to bend the conversation into another direction of misunderstandings and mistakes.

"What more do you want Mr Mahon?" asked Swinburne.

"I want prosecutions," I immediately replied. "It's a criminal offence to make a false crime report."

"This is the dichotomy if you like and let's cut to this. We've got Liz Keenan saying that you did swear and there was shouting…and she says the shouting is at her," said Swinburne, "we have a crime report saying there is swearing and aggression. But we also have the incident report and it doesn't actually talk about shouting or swearing in it. I've spoken to PC Thurston and what he relies on is the original notes. But you are quite right there's no mention of shouting and swearing. He doesn't want to mislead anybody so he can't remember anything."

"If there had have been shouting and swearing, he would have definitely remembered. It's only Liz who said I was shouting and swearing," I protested.

I was now becoming so frustrated with their attitude.

The conversation continued into who accused me of shouting and who didn't until I mentioned I had interviewed PC Hughes and I had also filmed the meeting. Ball and Swinburne suddenly stopped and looked at each other.

"You have a DVD? Well maybe we should look at it."

"Did he know he was being filmed?" asked Ball.

"No," I replied sharply, "I filmed the conversation to protect myself in case he would later accuse me of something else."

"This might be a good time to have a break and we could look at the DVD," suggested Ball.

"Good idea," said Simon.

I gathered up my papers, switched off my tape recorder and we were escorted back to the reception area. I suggested to Simon that we take a walk outside. It was a nice sunny day and I needed some air to help relieve me from the tension I was feeling. I was exhausted and didn't have confidence anymore about how the meeting was progressing. Simon suggested we write down the points that the two senior officers were being evasive about and try to get them to give proper answers.

We wrote a list of about six questions that we thought would put the two officers on the spot. When we went back into the reception area I sat watching two women arguing with a skinny little man about who he should be living with. I couldn't understand why they had brought him to the police station but it appeared from the conversation I overheard that they were trying to get him arrested for sleeping with both of them. Just as I was starting to become interested in the scenario we were called to return to the meeting.

Simon opened up with the first question about Allison Grundy withdrawing a meeting that had been arranged with Hughes and Thurston back in 2005 but they brushed that aside with, "we can't answer to why Mrs Grundy took that decision." Every question after that was met with silence. They sat there saying nothing. Ball then spoke.

"Well, can we just move on to your DVD? It was very helpful," said Ball, "I noticed you repeated the same question and PC Hughes did say he could not remember what was said or what he wrote."

"But he did say that I was calm that evening and didn't cause any fuss,"

I said.

They denied hearing that. I suggested they put the DVD back in the machine to confirm what Hughes actually said. They refused and continued saying that ex-PC Hughes couldn't remember what was said.

"You hear what you want to hear Mr Mahon."

"And you ignore what you don't want to hear," I replied.

We were getting nowhere. So I asked the question that would sum up the meeting.

"Are you actually sitting there and telling me you believe Liz?"

"I believe she has made a statement saying…," replied Ball.

"But is she telling the truth?"

"I've never met her," replied Ball.

"But from the evidence you've read, do you think she is telling the truth?"

"I can't make an assessment either way," said Ball.

"Well that's not concluding anything," I said, falling back into my chair with dismay.

I looked at Swinburne, "And what about you, are you saying the same?"

"I would go back to what the judge concluded," said Swinburne.

"Never mind what the judge concluded, do you believe her?"

"The judge said…"

"I'm not asking you what the judge said I'm asking you what do you think?"

"Are you now saying you're disagreeing with what the judge said?" asked Swinburne.

"Well," I stuttered but couldn't instantly think of a reply to the question so I said the first thing that came into my head, "…the evidence was so overwhelming the judge had no other option but to decide in my favour."

"I can't answer for the judge's actions but I will say this Mr Mahon, he has said the police are entitled to believe what Liz Keenan has told them. It is the judge saying that, not Hertfordshire Constabulary," insisted Swinburne.

"You've admitted Hertfordshire Constabulary have made a mistake, you've looked at the paper work, do you think Liz should be prosecuted for lying and wasting police time?"

"No." said Swinburne.

"So you think she is telling the truth?" I said again.

"I don't think she should be prosecuted for lying, no," said Swinburne, "I've seen a statement and based on the probabilities of what I've seen, I think there is truth in it, yes."

Silence hit the room for a moment and no one spoke.

"So you think that if this case was referred to the Crime Prosecution Services, it would not stack-up then?" said Simon.

"No." said Ball.

"The powers they were using at the time were wrong..." said Swinburne.

"And Liz had lied," I said.

"It was deliberately misleading," said Simon.

They didn't reply.

There was nothing more Simon and I could say. The officers' tactic was now to sit in silence. They were getting bored and wanted us to leave.

We left the meeting that afternoon, both of us with mixed feelings. Simon thought we had done well. The officers had promised to interview

Liz again but deep down inside I knew it was over. When we reached my car there was a parking ticket on it and I took that as another sign to stop pursuing the police for justice. We couldn't go into the Indian restaurant because it was closed but we did go and eat in the nearby shopping centre. I wanted to buy Simon a meal for all the help and support he had given.

When I received the written report from Swinburne, a few weeks later, it stated that the matter was closed. The police had questioned Liz again and come to the conclusion that she was telling the truth. Even though Superintendent Nicholls admitted Hughes had made a false crime report and the fact that three people had witnessed no aggression on the evening of the incident, the senior officers still maintain they believe Liz's version of events.

Liz had now made a new allegation that was a surprise to me and I found very hurtful. She told the police she had to sell the house in Hemel Hempstead because she was in fear of her safety from me. She had fought hard to keep our house and now 10 years after the incident, without ever seeing or speaking to me in that time, she was claiming that she had to sell it because of fear. When I read this new accusation I was astounded. I didn't imagine I could feel any more emotional pain from what Liz had already told the police but this was well below the belt. I couldn't understand why the police were quoting the accusation as if it was a fact. But then I could never understand why the police defended Liz for so long. The two officers, especially Hughes, had acted without thinking and their superiors defended them.

I did make enquiries with my solicitor and even met with my MP Mike Penning again to see if there was any legal way of challenging the police's decision but the financial cost could be high and the outcome could not be guaranteed. You can never get justice in this country without spending as much on the defence as the police spend on the prosecution. The police work for the prosecution. Everything is about winning not uncovering the truth. And they don't want to uncover the truth. Even if I won a Judicial Review against the police's decision, PC Hughes could not be prosecuted because (as the police informed me) he was out of the country. I did try to find out where he was but unsuccessfully. I couldn't even take a private prosecution against Liz because of the amount of time that had passed.

I went back to Hemel and met with my next door neighbour, John Hooper and we discussed how things had unexpectedly turned out for both of us. We agreed to meet before Christmas for a meal but a telephone call a month later from Neville's wife Lynn, informed me that John had suddenly taken ill and was in hospital. He died two weeks later from lung cancer on the day I intended to visit him.

It was now December 2014 and 10 years of my life, exactly to the month, had passed fighting the police because of one lie. Nick Hardwick, chairman of the IPCC's commissioners told the Big Issue magazine that it had taken too long. "*If the force had said to Mr Mahon back in Christmas 2004, 'Yes the officers have made a mistake and got the law wrong on this. We're really sorry, please accept our apologies', then this would never have come so far. The system itself is worse than what happened to him in the first place.*"

Almost half of the complaints against the police are for incivility or other neglects of duty. Relatively minor if taken alone but I was surprised to find that the scale of them is huge and few complaints brought against individual officers are upheld. According to the IPPC 89 per cent of the 14,558 complaints that it investigated in 2008 were rejected. It is rare for an officer to face criminal prosecution. Yet a police officer is arrested on suspicion of criminal offences almost every day, according to figures released under the freedom of information.

The best-known 2012 case is the 'Plebgate' affair involving PC Keith Wallis who was jailed for 12 months after being found out that he lied about witnessing shouting and swearing at the gates of Downing Street between former Tory chief whip, Andrew Mitchell and two police officers.

A crook is a crook but a police officer has a warrant card and a licence to commit a crime. Police officers get two weeks training and then assigned to a station with very little knowledge of the law.

I was just an ordinary citizen trying to expose a false accusation made against me.

I found to my detriment that the bad coppers lie and the good coppers stay silent. The financial cost to the police was totally unnecessary. I may have won my claim and that alone was worth the long hard fight but I didn't feel justice was served. PC Hughes may have lost his job over this incident but PC Thurston is still in the police force and Palfrey is still a magistrate.

As Mark Twain once said: *Twenty years from now you will be more disappointed by the things that you didn't do than by the ones you did.*

I'm glad that I fought the law and I'm glad that I didn't walk away. It would have been so much easier to give up but I didn't and I'm much happier now with the success I've achieved.

I threw a celebration party in the Boogaloo pub in Highgate, North London with a Rockabilly band playing and food prepared by Masako. Maureen presented me with a chocolate cake with '*I fought the law and won*' iced on top. It was a great night and worth every minute I had suffered suing the police. All my friends came and even my old friend Johnny Baker had travelled up from Brighton. One of the women at the party gave me a great big kiss when I told her 'I won my case'. She thought I had said 'I want my kiss'.

My daughter Jenna sent me a little note on Facebook that summed up my 10-year experience. 'Well done Dad'.

Mark Twain quoted: *A lie will make it around the world before the truth has time to put its shoes on.* Oh how I discovered that quote to be so true.

So never give up. If you put enough effort into something you want, you will achieve. The fight is worth it!

THE END